Conserving
Mount Nittany

A Dynamic Environmentalism

Conserving Mount Nittany

A Dynamic Environmentalism

Thomas A. Shakely

The Nittany Valley Society
State College

Published in the United States of America
by The Nittany Valley Society, Inc.
www.nittanyvalley.org

ISBN: 0-9853488-4-4
ISBN-13: 978-0-9853488-4-7

Conserving Mount Nittany: A Dynamic Environmentalism
Shakely, Thomas Anthony

The letters, op-eds, and editorials in "The Story of Hort Woods" appear
with permission from the *Centre Daily Times*.

"Who Owns Mount Nittany?" appears with permission. It was
originally published in 1976 in *Town & Gown*.

"The Mount Nittany Conservancy" appears with permission. It was
originally published in 2008 for Lion's Paw's Centennial celebration.

"The Legend of Mount Nittany" is excerpted from *The Legends of the
Nittany Valley*, published by The Nittany Valley Society.

"Hort Woods in Winter" appears on the back cover courtesy of The
Pennsylvania State University Archives. "The Hort Woods Ghost Walk"
appears courtesy of Pat Daugherty of The Tavern Restaurant.

Cover Photograph © William Ames | amesphotos.com
Back Photograph © Colin Gallagher | @colintgallagher
Cover Design by Jonathan Hartland

First Edition

To the natural dwelling places of the Great Spirit, amidst the asphalt canyons of man's progressive spirit.

Our Mountain

Mike Lynch

Across the silent Valley stands our
Mountain old and strong
Part of our college heritage
in story and in song

Through all the natural seasons we
watch her change her face
Shedding the white of winter
to green with gentle grace

In the heat of summer she gives
new leaves and wood
In the golden glow of autumn
her beauty is understood

What is it about this Mountain
with rugged rocks and rills
That gives we Penn Staters
a thousand prideful thrills

It's a sense of belonging to a school
that's part of us
In the annals of our lives
we count it as a plus

Today we pledge our loyalty
to our Mountain and Old State
By doing this we join our
founders strong and great

Contents

Introduction

A Dynamic Environmentalism

The story of Mount Nittany's conservation is the story of a people's extraordinary response to an ordinary Pennsylvania mountain. It is the basis for this extraordinary response with which the book of conversation and record is concerned. In explaining a "dynamic environmentalism" we will explore the means by which the people of Central Pennsylvania's Nittany Valley have shaped and conserved their environment.

The myths of the Mountain propagated by Henry W. Shoemaker and echoing through time in one form or another from our American Indian ancestors achieved something that can be considered a genuine miracle—creation (or, at least, conservation) *ex nihilo*. From the myths of Mount Nittany sprung the cultural basis for the reality of Mount Nittany as a sacred and exceptional site.

In *Popularizing Pennsylvania: Henry W. Shoemaker and the Progressive Uses of Folklore and History*, Dr. Simon J. Bronner explains Shoemaker's conservationist aim to "inspirit the land" not only as "a hedge against rapid industrialization" but also as a long term means to cultivate "civic values and regional pride."

Understanding dynamic environmentalism requires internalizing the vision of the early American conservationists, personalities as varied as President Theodore Roosevelt, Pennsylvania Governor Gifford Pinchot, Henry W. Shoemaker, and others like New York's William Canfield and Katherine Berry Judson of the Pacific Northwest.

The critical insight of these early environmentalists was the observation that the physical landscape is inextricably linked to the cultural landscape. Conservation of a physical thing was rarely achievable without a conservation of the feelings people had attached to it over time. A physical landscape might be beautiful, but only once it becomes inspirited within the cultural landscape can it become sacred and inviolable.

The process by which conservationists like Henry W. Shoemaker successfully "inspirited the land" of sites like Mount Nittany is worth exploring.

In a 1916 address to the National Institute of Arts and Letters, former president Theodore Roosevelt might as well have been outlining the vision of the American conservationists of his era. "The greatest work must bear the stamp of originality. ... American work must smack of our own soil, mental and moral, no less than physical, or it will have little of permanent value."

The American Indians were, really, the first naturalists in North America—not out of a mad affection for nature for nature's sake, but because they saw the spark of divinity animating their world. Our Indian ancestors had internalized, albeit naturally rather than intellectually, the same insights the early American conservationists sought to cultivate among the peoples of their own rapidly industrializing era.

"All art is mortal," writes Oswald Spengler, "not merely the individual artifacts, but the arts themselves. One day the last portrait of Rembrandt and the last bar of Mozart will have ceased to be—though possibly a colored canvas and a sheet of notes may remain—because the last eye and the last ear accessible to their message will have gone."

The philosophy of Spengler can be seen in the contrasting civilizations of the American Indian peoples and the Anglo-American pioneers. The former civilization, having seen the spark of the divine at work in the natural world, did not observe a landscape as simply so much air and soil and water. Rather, they had eyes and ears "accessible to the message" their divine landscapes communicated throughout the vast beauty of the continent. Their culture attuned them to see more than the equivalent of a colored canvas or a sheet of notes. Art was alive in the hills, streams, and valleys.

The story of our own civilization we know all too well. We still struggle to see the natural world as more than a canvas upon which to write the stories of economic gain or loss. We measure so much of the natural world in terms of its present utility. Seeing nature as a work of art to an American is a continual act of humility—of trying, of forgetting, and of occasional moments of awe and reverence.

It was, then, the great gift of the early conservationists to infuse our physical landscapes with a cultural depth sufficient to ensure the survival of both. This is what Henry W. Shoemaker achieved in the Nittany Valley perhaps more than any other place in Pennsylvania through his folklore. "Nita-Nee: A Tradition of a Juniata Maiden," appeared in his 1916 *Juniata Memories: Legends Collected in Central Pennsylvania*, and was likely the inspiration for an alternate student-crafted legend of Princess Nittany that appeared later that year in Penn State's student yearbook *LaVie*.

Shoemaker collected (and students shared) the cultural lore of the landscape, and it quickly came to shape the physical landscape—the intangibles of myth, lore, and tradition gave rise to a physical landscape tangibly molded by the ideas of the time. A spirit came to be seen as a part of the natural landscape.

"When we speak of the Nittany Valley," writes Christopher Buchignani in *The Legends of the Nittany Valley*, "we should recognize that the Indians were here first. They gave their names to the places we inhabit today—Nittany, Waupalani, and Bald Eagle, for example—and they gave voice to the spirit of the place. Later came the pioneering educators and students of what would become The Pennsylvania State University, who breathed in and gave form to that spirit, even naming themselves for it: They became the Nittany Lions."

In this we can see the local manifestation of Theodore Roosevelt's vision. In the Nittany Valley a culture of "permanent value" across generations of students and townspeople arose bearing a definite "stamp of originality" in the spirit of the place. The ethos of the Nittany Valley is firmly rooted in its "own soil, mental and moral, no less than physical" and has survived not only the glories of scholarly and athletic achievement but also the worst tragedy and most heinous sort of evil that a people can experience.

A spirit exists, in other words, that furnishes the basis for us to see the Nittany Valley as distinct from other valleys in the same way Oswald Spengler distinguished between recognizing a masterpiece as such from a mere collection of marks on a canvas.

Our cultural sentimentality, such as these feelings could very easily be reduced to, nonetheless impacts our physical landscape because it directs our civic policy. It guides our ecology because it determines how we think of our environment.

I am proposing that a dynamic environmentalism acts to preserve a *whole* landscape, and through this preservation of the entire reality of a particular environment it creates the cultural as well as the physical basis for an authentic conservationist spirit. Dynamic environmentalism can be understood most simply as an historically recovered sense of conservation that restores the fullness of its vision. A "static" environmentalism, by contrast, is an environmentalism that preserves only a fragment of a whole, living landscape. As such, it is an environmentalism worthy of praise, albeit one lacking a complete consciousness of the central purpose of the conservationist impulse.

When we infuse an unremarkable physical landscape—like Mount Nittany with its distinctively ordinary Pennsylvania rise and slope—with a distinctive spirit, the natural result is an extraordinary outcome. It is within this context, as I have written, that we can appreciate the story of Mount Nittany's conservation as the story of a people's extraordinary response to an ordinary Pennsylvania mountain.

If we understand the means by which the American conservationists sought to "inspirit the land," this question remains: Where can we look to find a cultural feeling capable of animating the sort of conservationist impulse that has conveyed Mount Nittany to us across time?

Simply put, the practical basis for conservation lies in an experience of history and place.

One does not really know much of what is really going on unless one enters into history, which starts by knowing the stories of your place—wherever you physically are. And while services like Wikipedia are increasingly distilling our history into digestible data sets, we still find ourselves delighted most viscerally through the narrative structure of story and parable. This is why folklore has proven itself as such a powerful delivery mechanism for a people's history.

Allow me to try to illustrate my point about the centrality of history and place to conservation by breaking the Fourth Wall— by speaking directly to you.

If I knew every *fact* there is about you—your age, height, weight, eye and hair color, birthplace, etc.—I really wouldn't know much about *you*. But, even if I never met you and didn't know any "facts" at all about you—if instead I listened to your roommate, your teammates, or your girlfriend or boyfriend tell me stories about you for an hour or so, then I think I would have a pretty good idea who you really are. Because it's in the stories about you that you really shine through.

The same is true for the place where you are. You don't really know a place until you hear how the people there talk about it, and hear the stories they tell about it. Until you know those stories, Mount Nittany and the Nittany Valley will be just like any other place in our globalized civilization—so much convenient niceness to be utilized and forgotten.

It's only if we enter into the stories of a specific history and place that we'll have the context for the conservation that ensures the "permanent value" of Theodore Roosevelt's America.

If there's a larger point to the centrality of history and place to conservation, it's that facts alone are not enough. No information campaign will, by itself, ensure the success of an environmental campaign. Facts alone are a raw material—practically useless without a creative spirit to provide context and distill their essential nature.

The biographies of great men and women rarely turn on the factual simplicities of their lives, but rather on singular moments of importance when their fate seems to become inevitable—when the choices of life fall away in pursuit of a destiny. The stories of our physical places, our cities, towns, and communities, develop in the same way. Their evolution is not the result of dispassionate environmental processes, but rather are the result of complex and often messy choices we make individually and collectively about who we say we are and what we choose to become.

In the Nittany Valley, we've chosen to become a people who revere Mount Nittany and who hold it in trust for successive generations. We've chosen to learn the history of our place in the hopes that those who come after us follow our example, as we've tried to follow the example of those who came before us—from

Coach Bill O'Brien all the way back to founders like Evan Pugh and George Atherton.

How do we explain the weight of meaning we attach to our cultural history? How do we explain what it means to look at Mount Nittany and think of its legendary rising to serve as a barrier against the "wicked winds of the north"? We know that it is only a fable—a fabulous story that never happened in any scientific reality. Yet it is *our* story. The stories of the Mountain belong to us and no one else, and it makes that Mountain belong to us in a way that it can never belong to any outsiders, no matter how much scientific knowledge they may have.

That is why there have been such spectacular efforts by the people of the Nittany Valley to preserve Mount Nittany in its natural state. These have included the incorporation of the Lion's Paw Alumni Association in 1945 to buy up 525 acres on the face and top of the Mountain to prevent the land from being logged and the creation of the Mount Nittany Conservancy in 1981 to buy up even more of the Mountain to prevent it from being developed. These two groups together have dedicated themselves to preserving and conveying a cultural spirit specific to the University and the Nittany Valley.

We maintain Mount Nittany as a sacred trust through these groups and other efforts because we appreciate the worth of encouraging every student and townsperson to make his or her own personal hike on Mount Nittany. We want people, especially newcomers, to make their own pilgrimage to a source of our spirit. In this way we strengthen our community through ritual and common experience.

I hope I have succeeded in conveying the meaning of conservation as an environmentalism of both the cultural and physical environment.

We know, at a minimum, that the legends of Princess Nittany have had the direct result that the Nittany Mountain is today neither a housing development nor a lumbering tract. We know that one bit of nature is preserved unspoiled within walking distance of the campus for climbing and pleasure.

In the conversation with Dr. Ben Novak that forms the core of this book, I have sought to ferret out not merely the practical strategies and tactics that have preserved Mount Nittany, but also to convey the intangible basis for its conservation and the feelings of affection that so many in the Nittany Valley have for the Mountain.

In any history of Mount Nittany, the contemporary reader will be at a severe disadvantage without having encountered Terry Dunkle's masterful 1976 *Town & Gown* profile of the personalities instrumental to Mount Nittany's early preservation. I'm deeply grateful for Mr. Dunkle's enthusiastic support and permission to include his excellent piece in this book.

A substantial portion of this book is also devoted to the story of Hort Woods, which is the story of a failure to preserve an historic place on the University's campus. Hort Woods, had this ancient, once-sweeping forest been conserved in its natural state, would be well positioned to serve as an even more local counterpart to Mount Nittany for the students of Penn State. Imagine a vast and venerable forest *right on campus* for experiencing the sort of serenity and beauty that today only a trip to Lemont can promise. This would be something extraordinary.

The story of Hort Woods is, instead, the story of a place never sufficiently inspirited to be widely recognized as sacred and inviolable. An environmental effort to preserve the Woods was waged over time, but lacking the dynamism of the complete conservationist ethic, the effort failed and the Woods yielded to the practical demands of the age. Hort Woods survives in diminished form as something closer to a professionally managed memorial than a genuine woodland forest.

An experience of Hort Woods as anything like an experience of Mount Nittany is today impossible. It lives on in name, surviving abstractly somewhere in the recesses of our cultural memory. We know Evan and Rebecca Pugh and George Atherton and other founders traversed both the wilds of Mount Nittany and the vastness of Hort Woods—but it is nearly impossible to experience the serenity of whatever they must have encountered in the Hort Woods of today. It remains possible, fortunately, to experience the same quiet moments of awe or contemplation they, too, must have enjoyed on the Mountain.

To make the short walk through the Hort Woods of our time, conversely, is to never shake the sight of asphalt, brick, and concrete, or the sound of nearby traffic, or the rumble of heating and cooling units. It is a conscious experience of the effort to lose civilization on the campus rather than the effortless loss of yourself amidst the sprawling nature of the Mountain. Invariably, the piercing lighting of the campus at nighttime or its audible rumblings during daylight only serve to highlight the thinness of what remains.

It is a paradox that both the University and the Common-wealth of Pennsylvania, the cultural and civic infrastructure designed to exist as far into the future as we can imagine, have been poorer stewards of Hort Woods than private citizens have been conservers of Mount Nittany through voluntary association and effort. There is a lesson here about the institutions, methods, and persons we consider timeless.

Mount Nittany and Hort Woods tell dramatically different stories, and it is hoped that the record presented in this book can shed light on how two preservation efforts within the same generation could yield such different results.

In considering the practicality of the "dynamic environmentalism" of conservation, a lingering question remains. Can anything be done to cultivate a receptivity among a people to a conservationist ethos? In other words, can anything be done to ensure a people will have "eyes and ears receptive to the message" of the worth of their place?

The implicit aim of any conservation effort is the preservation of something beautiful precisely so that its beauty can continue to bring joy to the people. In other words, a conservationist ethos is perhaps more properly understood as a cultural *eros*—a spirit of affection shared amongst a people. In the context of this *eros* a diverse people can come to see themselves as part of a common story and their action (or inaction) as contributing to the unfolding narrative that will define their community. I believe, therefore, the answer lies in demonstrating an authentic concern for the people to whom you're speaking rather than for the abstract thing you wish to preserve.

Maya Angelou captures this thinking with her famous observation that "people will forget what you said" but will "never forget how you made them feel."

I still remember the way I felt as a boy growing up in Pennsylvania's Bucks County in the 1990s. As one of the early members of the Millennial Generation, my childhood was one of the last of the pre-internet, and relatedly, the pre-monitoring era. I didn't think of this until much later, but growing up the doors to our home were never locked. In summers I was free to use my time more or less as I saw fit, and during school months the hours between dismissal and dinner were largely my own.

Ours was a typical suburban neighborhood, but there was a woods across the street from our home. As far as I know it had no name. I spent countless hours over late mornings, afternoons, and evenings in the final moments before the era of continuous communication alone under the trees. The light casting shadows at odd angles and the creative mind of my childhood-self supplying adventures that in spirit carried me far from the physical scene.

Our home was without climate control. On summer nights every window would be open, the warm breeze saturating the settling house. The nearby woods performed a nightly symphony best enjoyed on the porch near my grandfather—himself a Penn Stater of the Class of 1950. I can still see him smoking his pipe over some book or other. The roar of cicadas throughout the brush and the cooing of owls perched in high places linger in my memory, infused with the sweet scent of burning tobacco. June bugs are still fumbling their way toward the light of the porch. I'm still that child in awe of the grandeur of the outdoors, to which no activity other than appreciation can enhance.

It was within this context of a tame suburb that retained a bit of its wild heritage that a love was kindled over time. I carry many of the habits of my youth into the present, though it's true that it's more difficult to escape climate controls and less frequent that I can leave a door or window freely open. It is within the context of the liberty of my childhood that I particularly cherish the liberty afforded still by Mount Nittany and places like it.

For the rising generations, who will likely rarely experience the type of liberty of my childhood, I can only hope that the inviolability of our Nittany Mountain continues to abide and that the spirit of the Nittany Valley survives as a living force among the people of the valley.

Thomas A. Shakely
Philadelphia

I.

The Legends of the Mountain and Early Preservation

Entering the Nittany Valley is something of a special experience for many, whether a young man just about to begin his freshman year, a new townsperson-settler coming to make a career, a home, and a family, or simply a visitor coming for time among friends. It's not simply that the Borough of State College, for instance, is a lovely little college town. I think, rather, that there's a natural sense that the Nittany Valley is a distinct phenomenon.

The mountains of Central Pennsylvania are probably most responsible for this. The sprawling geography of Pennsylvania's Delaware Valley isn't something that's felt in the same way. The hills and ridges just aren't as pronounced there. But coming into Central Pennsylvania, especially through the narrow, winding corridors of Interstate 80 or Interstate 99, still impresses upon you the reality that you've left wherever you started and that you're traversing a fresh territory.

Mount Nittany lends to the Nittany Valley its most obvious character and force, pressing itself gently upon its admirers as not merely the namesake of the valley it cradles in its shadow, but as the symbol of the place, too.

"The mountain is the most distinctive single object in our landscape," observed Fred Lewis Pattee in 1922. Its "melodious name" ever more becomes "a unique Penn State possession." For Pattee, Mount Nittany was a "sentinel" lending protection and a beautiful grace "at the extreme flank of the range overlooking the magnificent valley."

Whatever the precise story of the Nittany Valley, and whether scientific inquiry one day confirms there's "something in the water" to make Happy Valley so happy, Mount Nittany meanwhile stands as the symbol of the spirit, loyalty, and magnetic, inexplicable pull so many feel upon entering the valley.

"Our mountain bears no oil," Terry Dunkle notes in his 1976 *Town & Gown* profile of Mount Nittany. It "hides no diamonds or gold." Indeed, Mount Nittany is an ordinary Pennsylvania mountain. "The prospect of buying her would give goose bumps to none but the most sentimental of real estate agents." Yet, inexplicably, the Mountain calls to us: "Nittany's value is not to be measured in dollars, but in the dark whisperings of the heart."

A curiosity about the nature of these "whisperings of the heart" is what prompted the conversations with Dr. Ben Novak that comprise this book.

Thomas A. Shakely: Starting with proper introductions, Dr. Ben Novak, you were a resident of Centre County for more than three decades, you're a four-term former Penn State Trustee, and you're the founder of the Mount Nittany Conservancy.

Born in Johnstown, Pennsylvania on Feb. 15, 1943, you graduated from The Pennsylvania State University in 1965, served as student body president your senior year, and were a brother at Tau Kappa Epsilon. In 1968 you graduated from Georgetown University Law Center. From 1968-70 you served as a Captain in the U.S. Army, Infantry in Vietnam where you won the Bronze Star.

You were admitted to the Bar of Pennsylvania, and practiced law for more than 30 years with your own firm in State College and Bellefonte. You've served as an adjunct professor and assistant dean of students and as president of Lion's Paw Alumni Association. In 1999 you earned your Ph.D. from Penn State in philosophy, history, and political science.

You've long mentored students, advised civic efforts, and sought a renewal in University life according to the vision of Evan Pugh and the founders of the University for many years.

In a distilled sense, you've lived much of your life in the shadow of Mount Nittany. It is the Mountain and its story, of course, that concern our purposes here.

Mount Nittany is regarded as a sort of special mountain to the people of Centre County and to Penn Staters especially. Yet to any outsider it would look like little more than an unremarkable Pennsylvania mountain. I'm curious to hear first: What is Mount Nittany? What makes it special? Why do people visit it almost in the way pilgrims visit holy sites? Why does it capture our imagination?

Ben Novak: Well, let me just first reinforce your central idea that Mount Nittany is not a particularly outstanding geological feature. It's just another Pennsylvania mountain.

There's this story of a visiting student from another university somewhere out West who came to State College. "I've heard about this famous Nittany mountain," he remarks. "Show it to me." So the locals point over to Mount Nittany, and the visiting student retorts, "That's not Nittany mountain. That's Not-*any* mountain." After all, compared to the mountains of the West, it's just a hill.

Yet from the very beginning of Penn State's history—and in fact even before that—there was something considered sacred about Mount Nittany.

It was the subject of several legends about a Princess Nit-A-Nee, and these legends existed over time and have come down through our American Indian ancestors to our settler ancestors, and finally now to us. Nittany Mountain was known to the Indians and considered a sacred place, in other words. So the feeling of Mount Nittany as something special and holy predates even Penn State's founding.

When Evan Pugh arrived in the Nittany Valley in the 1850s to establish what would become Penn State, we know from records that he took students camping on Mount Nittany. It was on the Mountain that our first president made his famous "Evan Pugh Venison Stew." The Mountain from our earliest days was a place for camping, a place for looking out over the valley, a place for being with others.

So it has had this aura of sacredness from the very beginning —certainly from Evan Pugh's day as a place of adventure and fellowship, and it seems so even in the long unrecorded days of the American Indians who mythologized the Mountain.

This aura seems to have taken on an even greater life from Penn State's founding to the early 20th century when Henry W. Shoemaker published his legends of Princess Nit-A-Nee, and disseminated the legend-stories he writes of having heard from aged American Indians, settlers, and others across Pennsylvania in what was then still often like lingering frontier territories.

These legendary origin stories speak of Mount Nittany rising over the grave of Princess Nit-A-Nee, or of being the result of the Great Spirit-God memorializing a fallen champion. Princess Nit-A-Nee is described as a great leader of the Indians, who, when her father dies, inherits the tribe and leads it to victory over invading Southern tribes, recapturing the area and deciding to settle permanently in what we know as the Nittany Valley today.

The legends tell also of the Mountain being a gift from the Great Spirit, the Gitchie Manitou, having arisen to prevent the Wicked Wind of the North from coming down across the plains, ripping out the vital food crops. So Nit-A-Nee's name was in time given the meaning of "the barrier against the wind" or "windbreak" because the Mountain rose over her grave to prevent the North wind from destroying the people of the valley.

Henry W. Shoemaker's publication of these legendary stories that were apparently being passed orally among the people for generations was a critical point in the history of the Mountain as our present era of mass communications was just dawning.

TAS: Since you mention Henry W. Shoemaker, let's leave the Nittany Valley for a moment as a means to come back to the story of the Mountain. Shoemaker is a fascinating figure—as a journalist-publisher in Pennsylvania he's an early version in some sense of what Joseph Mitchell, I think, became at *The New Yorker* in terms of someone who flitted amongst the people, listening, recording, and sharing their stories.

If Shoemaker's remembered today it's probably most often for having become Pennsylvania's first State Folklorist—but he was a genuine Renaissance man as not only a writer and folklorist, but also conservationist, historian, and diplomat.

Joseph Mitchell, meanwhile, told New York City's story in such a masterful and humane way—reminiscent of Shoemaker's folk stories. Mitchell's 1943 *New Yorker* profile of McSorely's Old Ale House, "McSorely's Wonderful Saloon" is extraordinary. An East Village watering hole older than Penn State itself, McSorely's still hums just off Cooper Square, and hardly without having changed from either Mitchell's day or its founding. I always liked e.e. cumming's ode to McSorely's, the place with "the ale which never lets you grow old." Sometimes I think of this when I'm in the Nittany Valley, watching as all of us who are aging drink alongside the perennially youthful students.

Shoemaker and Mitchell were distinct in terms of their generational character, but both sought to convey the personas and narratives of their communities in a simple, unvarnished way.

What was it that Shoemaker found in the Nittany Valley?

BN: Your comparison is a good one. Henry W. Shoemaker took a position he learned from the masters of his own time. Remember, Shoemaker is on the scene just as Grimm's Fairy Tales and the stories of Hans Christian Andersen are catching fire and becoming especially popular in Europe. Well, Shoemaker felt that there were as many and as wonderful legends in the forests of Pennsylvania as there were in the Black Forest of Germany. And so he traveled around Pennsylvania—much like you point out Joseph Mitchell later did in New York City—stopping in the general stores and in the pubs and hotels and so forth to gather those stories. And he would go back to his room, write those stories down, and publish them in newspapers like the *Altoona Tribune*. Serial-features were popular back then, and so his legend-stories would appear weekly. Later he would assemble collections and publish them in books.

Think of one of Shoemaker's remarks that's featured in "The Legends of the Nittany Valley" and on its back cover:

"There is no spot of ground a hundred feet square in the Pennsylvania mountains that has not its legend. Some are old, as ancient as the old, old forests. Others are of recent making or in formation now. Each one is different, each is full of its own local color."

Well, Mount Nittany for Shoemaker was exactly such a thing; a fertile spot of ground whose story deserved telling. His most famous Nit-A-Nee legend appears in his 1916 book "Juniata Memories," and it's certainly no coincidence that Penn Staters published a version of the Princess Nittany legend—their own, unique version—in the 1916 *LaVie*, the student yearbook.

The students re-wrote the story in the language of that time, which was much more flowery than Shoemaker's original version. But even before 1916 the story of the Mountain had become central to Penn State and the area.

In the 1920s the students started talking about putting up a big concrete "S" on the face of the Mountain for "State," and one of the professors—actually, Fred Lewis Pattee, author of our Alma Mater—squelched that, saying that it would be a hideous scar. This was a time when professors really influenced students' thinking in more than simply a personal way. And really from that point on, preserving Mount Nittany in its natural state became the ideal, and the Mountain in its plain beauty became firmly a symbol of Penn State.

TAS: In the span of essentially a decade you've got students writing their own origin story, mythologizing Mount Nittany in *LaVie* and on the other hand in just a few years they want to brand the Mountain with slabs of concrete. This rather beautifully encapsulates human nature, doesn't it? Feeling a deep affection for something or someone, and yet wanting to "improve" it by leaving your mark on it?

The earliest informal, public preservation of Mount Nittany can be seen as Pattee's declaration of support for the Mountain's natural beauty—leaving the lands as they might have been thousands of years beforehand, even before the time of Princess Nittany.

Our contemporary motives would be primarily ecological or environmentally concerned, but it seems like beauty for its own sake drove this earliest spirit of conservation. Or was the environmental concern as we might recognize it presently a force then, too?

BN: As far as I know, ecological and environmental concerns played little role in the 1920s. It was likely a combination of three things at work in the public mind: (1) the natural enjoyment of the natural area, (2) the mythological import of the Nit-A-Nee legends combined with the idea of the Mountain as a sacred site, and (3) the historical attitude of tying Mount Nittany to the American Indians by preserving the land in an un-improved way.

Remember that back then Penn State and State College were in the middle of a rural area—there as really nothing nearby. We were far from any big towns or cities, and so everything was virgin land. This explains why the idea of environmental concerns never occurred to students or townspeople. But it did have its sacred meaning, its legendary meaning, its symbolic meaning to Penn Staters even beyond the ability to enjoy hiking and wandering.

What I'm trying to get across when I talk about Mount Nittany's "sacredness" is this: It seems as if people felt there was a spirit in the Mountain that we didn't just invent. It's always been there, they felt. The Indians had felt it, and we picked it up.

I don't think anyone would have thought of it exactly this way back then, but the way I think of it now is that the feeling of the students and townspeople for Mount Nittany worked to forge a cross-generational and cross-cultural spirit.

By the way, in the early part of the 20th century Mount Nittany was clear-cut. You can find pictures of the bald

Mountain if you know where to look. The timber was needed for the iron furnace at Centre Mansion; it was needed to build up Pennsylvania and the West, and the lumber would be run down the rivers, sending it all over. So when students were talking about putting that concrete "S" on the face of Mount Nittany, the new growth was just beginning. By the 1940s, that growth had come up pretty well and it could be cut again and it was this reality that furnished the basis for Lion's Paw Alumni Association to step into the situation—but we're getting a bit ahead of ourselves.

TAS: Alright. You've mentioned Lion's Paw and this common "cross-generational" spirit for the Mountain. Lion's Paw was itself a group that had formed, along with maybe a dozen other class-specific honor societies all roughly in the same time period of the first two decades of the 20th century.

Students write their *LaVie* ode to the Mountain in 1916 at the same time that Henry W. Shoemaker's own origin story had been in print in one form of another for at least a few years. Pattee puts down the "S"-improvement in the early 1920s. The Depression hits, then World War II intervenes a few years later.

But roughly only a generation after Pattee's defense of the natural beauty of the Mountain, it's once again in peril of defacement. Explain how we reach this point, and the role of Lion's Paw in the first act of actual land preservation.

BN: Lion's Paw was formed in 1908, and rose out of the tumult of the 1905 student strike. This student strike is a remarkable part of Penn State's history, and thanks to George Atherton's wisdom and the exemplary insight of students, the strike resulted in our first student government and constituency groups like the honor societies that you mentioned.

Lion's Paw is a senior-class honor society, and is one of the few surviving honor societies. It arose in the early 20th century out of this student strike as a means to cultivate leaders, and it had counterparts in the form of societies for juniors, sophomores, and freshmen. Few of these societies have survived, and those that have survived seem today to act more as secretive societies than honor societies, so their influence among students is not as great.

Yet Lion's Paw has been a tremendously successful example of what these societies sought to do, which could be understood in its simplest form as "building up Penn State". In the early days its members were known by all on the campus, and because of this they could be looked to for leadership and they tended to take their responsibility seriously even after graduation.

In 1945, an advertisement was sent to the *Centre Daily Times*. It announced that a large part of Mount Nittany was being put up for sale—some 525 acres over the top and along the sides of the Mountain. Bill Ulerich, a local Lion's Paw alumnus who also happened to be editor of the newspaper at the time, saw this advertisement and received word that West Virginia Pulp and Paper was going to buy Mount Nittany to start clear cutting it again. So Bill called up his friends Russell Clark and Ridge Riley, who was involved with Lion's Paw alumni. They met in the office of Wayland Dunaway, a local attorney and another Lion's Paw member, and decided they were going to buy that land. So they signed an Agreement of Sale in their names and decided to form a corporation that could take responsibility for the land, and so Lion's Paw Alumni Association, Inc. came into existence.

TAS: This is the moment, then, when Lion's Paw goes from strictly student honor society, a campus organization, to something that exists independently, with alumni taking prominent, explicit leadership roles for the conservation of the Mountain. Is this the same Wayland Dunaway, by the way, who wrote the 1946 book "History of the Pennsylvania State College", Penn State's first official history?

BN: I believe this Wayland Dunaway was either the son or even grandson of the Dunaway who wrote the history book.

The Dunaways are an example of the old-time sort of families that have been a part of the Nittany Valley community for so long. When I first began practicing law in Central Pennsylvania I felt as if I would have to live three lifetimes before I could ever be considered anything like the sort of Penn Staters whose family names were synonymous with the town. In our globalized world, where we've become so used to picking up and moving every few years, and so disconnected from where we live, I find that simply because I've retained small bits of that old-time attitude, some younger people view people like me as folks who've just always been here. But the Dunaways have been a great family—playing a role both in the making and recording of our history.

And as you mention, it was unique that Lion's Paw Alumni Association, Inc. formed as it did—as an alumni group.

When Bill, Russell, and the others they worked with formed LPAA, they sent out letters for money to make good on their commitment. Eventually they got the money, and this is the short version of how Lion's Paw alumni came to own 525 acres of Mount Nittany. After they bought the land they really worked to preserve it, stopping power lines from going across it, keeping mischief-makers away, paying the taxes on it. It very quickly became a great, common effort.

TAS: Terry Dunkle paints a more complete portrait of the the story of Mount Nittany's early preservation in his 1976 *Town & Gown* article "Who Owns Mount Nittany?"

Lion's Paw buys 525 acres, and in time the Mount Nittany Conservancy buys a few hundred more—so today there are more than 800 protected acres. For perspective, how large it the total Mountain acreage?

BN: If the Mount Nittany Conservancy and others could rally, making friendships and continuing the purchasing efforts, we would probably want to buy another 1,000 acres on the sides of the Mountain. This would cover most of what everybody thinks of when they think of Mount Nittany.

TAS: We're about to get into the Mount Nittany Conservancy in earnest, but I'm curious to hear if there's anything else worth adding about the early preservation efforts.

BN: I think of it this way: In the 1910s and '20s there was a spirit in the air, a spirit felt for Mount Nittany. It was a spirit lingering from the era of the American Indians, and carried on by those surviving in the area and conveyed to American settlers. Henry W. Shoemaker picked up on the spirit by telling the stories he was hearing and sharing them with new generations, like the Penn Staters who loved his story of Nit-A-Nee so much that they re-wrote in in *LaVie*. This spirit was in the air, so anyone could breathe it in. Professors like Pattee breathed it in, students writing their *LaVie* legend breathed it in, and by the 1940s when the Mountain was threatened in a serious way Lion's Paw alumni breathed it in.

So from 1945 onward there appeared articles almost every year in the *Centre Daily Times* and so forth telling of actions Lion's Paw was taking to prevent any defacing of the Mountain and preserving it. Lion's Paw became the keeper of the Mountain —not simply because they owned it, but because they loved it. After all, it was their love for it in the first place that led them almost entirely on faith to make that purchase.

Of all personalities most intimately connected with Mount Nittany, Mike Lynch was one who was always up on that Mountain checking out everything, really loving it.

Mike Lynch was a Lion's Paw member and became the most visible "Keeper of the Mountain." Every year he gave his famous Lion's Paw "Mountain Report." Now, this report would sometimes last as long as two hours. Hearing that today, you figure, "Boy, that would bore everybody!" But no—it was the height of every meeting. People would travel to that meeting *just* to listen to Mike give his Mountain Report. He wasn't charismatic or articulate, but he would talk about Mount Nittany with so much love that no one was going to miss it.

It was a fantastic thing. Mike loved the Mountain so much— he built his house so he could always look at it. When he was in the hospital he had to be on the proper side of the building so he could look on it. Everything he did was Mount Nittany, and this spirit infected the entire board and the entire body of alumni and students.

I was one of those who picked up the spirit and feeling for Mount Nittany from Mike Lynch and others from the early era.

II.

The Rise of the
Mount Nittany Conservancy

If the story of Mount Nittany's early preservation is that of a small group coming together to act as stewards for the Nittany Valley's common symbol, the rise of the Mount Nittany Conservancy is the story of the Nittany Valley's response to both crisis and opportunity.

"All things human, in time, go badly." Ever since first hearing it, this small piece of common wisdom has stuck with me. At first, it might seem like simple pessimism. It's not pessimism, though. It's humility. It's a powerful reminder for me that the works of man are neither perfect nor perfectible. We can never be too cocksure or comfortable with the things we create.

I think part of the genius of those who conserve Mount Nittany is the desire to preserve the Mountain in its natural state. In doing so, we have chosen not to mark the Mountain with "things human" that will "in time, go badly." We let the Mountain be the Mountain. It radiates beauty because it is beautiful. There is nothing we can do as man to improve what nature has given us except to ensure nature the free space to be naturally herself.

Yet even as Mount Nittany safely passed through time to the people of the Nittany Valley for informal protection in the 1920s and formal preservation in the 1940s, the man-made structures for the Mountain's conservation proved not quite as timeless or perfect as her natural beauty.

As the Nittany Valley grew through the late 20th century, the historic keepers of Mount Nittany reached a period of change, challenge, and opportunity in the 1970s. New lands were coming up for sale even at the same time that some Lion's Paw alumni considered discontinuing their efforts due to financial strain.

Yet the allure of Mount Nittany—or perhaps it was the spirit of Nit-A-Nee dwelling in the Nittany Valley—had whispered to many hearts over the years. The wisdom of American naturalist John Muir, perhaps especially to be expected for people in a college town, had embedded itself in the form of a conviction for conserving the Mountain as a special treasure for all to share.

"Wilderness is a necessity," asserts Muir to S. Hall Young in the 1915 "Alaska Days with John Muir." Muir laments of a life merely of work: "I am losing precious days. I am degenerating into a machine for making money. I am learning nothing in this trivial world of men. I must break away and get out into the mountains to learn the news."

We all feel these stirring within us in those moments when the shadows cast by a thousand serious things are waxing even as the fortifying light of day is waning. Thanks to Lion's Paw, generations of students and a full generation of townspeople had come to know Mount Nittany, finding that even on their worst days they had a place close by to "break away" and "learn the news" of the world outside of simply man's concerns.

The entire Nittany Valley community came to share the spirit of Lion's Paw and Fred Lewis Pattee and Henry W. Shoemaker and the American Indians for their Mountain, even as the elite keepers of the Mountain felt less able than ever to meet the challenge and opportunities of the moment.

It was in this context that the Mount Nittany Conservancy came to be. The Conservancy would represent a reincarnation of Lion's Paw's efforts to preserve the Mountain, albeit in a broader way that would solve pressing challenges while also enabling new swaths of the Mountain to be added to the preservation effort.

The first formal preservation of Mount Nittany took place with the initiative of an elite few who possessed a feeling for the Mountain. The second wave of formal preservation would draw upon the spirit of a whole community—not an *aristos*, but a *demos*.

Mount Nittany is what is seen. The Mount Nittany Conservancy is the force that is unseen. In the following conversation with Dr. Novak, we will explore the formation of this unseen force that has come to channel the spirit of a people.

TAS: Dr. Novak, you arrive on campus as a freshman in 1961, and by your senior year in 1965 you've been elected Student Body President and are a part of Lion's Paw. So by the time of your graduation, we're only a single generation removed from Lion's Paw Alumni Association's original purchase of 525 acres of the Mountain. Walk us through what's happening when you arrive back in the Nittany Valley after Vietnam to practice law and renew your acquaintance with the town and university. You had become involved with Lion's Paw Alumni Association by this point, correct?

BN: Once I settled back in town I worked for a time with Ray Murphy, who was Dean of Students and who wrote to me when I was in Vietnam. It was Ray who convinced me to avoid graduate school by letting me know I had a job waiting for me in the Nittany Valley as Assistant Dean of Students. This is how I came back, and ultimately started practicing law here.

I struck up friendships and relationships with the older attorneys and professors and so forth, because that's how I was raised to think about settling in a place—that you've got to get to know everyone and know the place and be a part of things. In this sense becoming involved with the Lion's Paw Alumni Association was a natural decision.

It was in 1975 or thereabouts that a landowner on the Mountain came to us who had some 213 acres that he wanted to sell. This landowner had bought them maybe five or 10 years before for, I think, $25 an acre. Anyway, when he decided he wanted to sell he came first to Lion's Paw Alumni Association to make an offer. I was on the board at that time as treasurer.

The LPAA board considered the offer, which put the cost at about $50 an acre, and decided that we couldn't afford it—that it was too much for us.

The cost would have been around $10,000, but understand that at this time LPAA was having trouble raising even the few hundred dollars from its alumni body of 600 or so that it needed each year to pay the taxes on its Mount Nittany landholdings. So this was the context for why even this good offer didn't seem feasible at the time, and why the board decided we couldn't raise that kind of money.

As a matter of fact, one day the officers of LPAA had a meeting during my time as treasurer, and I was there in Steve Garban's office when we talked about disbanding Lion's Paw Alumni Association, Inc. because we didn't think we could raise the money to operate.

TAS: Your point about "settling in a place" and getting to know the elders, so to speak, strikes me as both strategically on-point and generally lovely. It's human.

Speaking of the Nittany Valley as a place worth settling into reminds me of a book by Rod Dreher I just picked up. It's called *The Little Way of Ruthie Leming*, and it's about his sister's life and death in St. Francisville, Louisiana. Dreher talks about returning to St. Francisville when his sister is diagnosed with cancer and seeing the warmth and support of the family. Dreher wonders "whether the ordinary life Ruthie led in their country town was in fact a path of hidden grandeur, even spiritual greatness, concealed within the modest life of a mother and teacher." I think of the Nittany Valley and the "ordinary life" of so many townspeople, professors, alumni, and others. I think there's certainly a hidden grandeur here that no marketing effort could quite properly convey.

A lot of places possess a sort of "hidden grandeur," probably, but the larger the town or city the harder it is to encounter the virtues of a place in a personal way, in the way you did when you came back to town.

Let's shift back to our story. If your personal experience with LPAA was so characterized by uncertainty, how do we make the leap from talk about disbanding to rapid new land acquisition? What was your experience with buying land on the Mountain?

BN: I thought it was a terrible shame to pass that $10,000 opportunity by, because it was an incredible deal. Wilhelm Kogelmann, another Mountain landowner who had a home on the Mountain, ended up stepping in and buying that land we turned down at the cost of $50 an acre. At the time I said that we never should have passed that up, but I was new and young and went along with the older people on the board and trusted their judgment.

But once Willy Kogelmann bought that land, things started to happen. Mr. Kogelmann started putting up boundary markers and "No Trespassing" signs. It was his land now, of course, but this presented a real problem in that a major route for Lion's Paw and its actives passed through his new property on the Mountain coming up from Boalsburg. So this drastically affected Lion's Paw, not to mention the historic purpose of LPAA's ownership of the Mountain as "public property privately owned" for all to enjoy.

As this was happening we heard about a piece of land that was owned by the Lee Estate—Christopher Lee's family of Boalsburg and the Lee Mansion fame. The Lee Estate owned 30 acres on the Mountain and offered to sell it for, I think, about $1,000 an acre.

As a lawyer, I knew that by buying these 30 land-locked acres LPAA would then automatically acquire a legal right-of-way to get to these new acres. In other words, this would counter Mr. Kogelmann's "No Trespassing" signs and allow us access to the Mountain in our normal way of getting up there.

The LPAA board said, "Alright Ben, let's see if you can raise the money." This was 1977 or '78. So I sent out a letter as treasurer to the 600 or so alumni, and I was amazed because I got telephone calls and letters from alumni saying, in effect, "Ben, do anything you need. We'll guarantee the money." It was amazing— the response to save and preserve Mount Nittany in its natural state. I knew from this experience that there was a vast reservoir of goodwill and fundraising ability, because we raised that money rather quickly and bought those 30 acres from the Lees.

Shortly after this, there was another landowner who had two acres and a cabin on Mount Nittany, right along the same route from Boalsburg. He had a right-of-way to the cabin, and our own right-of-way would take us to the top of Mount Nittany from the cabin. He offered to sell the two acres and cabin for $20,000. So, I went back to the LPAA board and said, "Let's buy this too." I sent out more letters. The alumni responded just as readily, and we ended up raising a total of $50,000 for these two purchases in a relatively short time.

These experiences led me to guess that we were seeing just the tip of the iceberg in terms of the community's feeling for Mount Nittany, because at this time we were raising these funds solely from Lion's Paw alumni. We were speaking to only a small portion of the community.

TAS: If you were experiencing success with raising funds using Lion's Paw Alumni Association, what led you to believe the Mount Nittany Conservancy was the best model for the future? It seems like the "if it ain't broke, don't fix it" mentality would come into play here.

BN: At this time, although the Lion's Paw Alumni Association was incorporated as a non-profit corporation, it did not yet have 501(c)(3) tax-exempt status. The Mount Nittany Conservancy was created specifically to obtain such status. Part of the deal with Willy Kogelmann was that he would sell part of the 213 acres, and donate the other, provided that the purchaser had tax-exempt status. Similarly, to raise the amount of funds necessary to buy the acres being sold, the Conservancy would be the more practical way to attract large donations. But this is to jump ahead a bit, so let me explain.

As the 1980s dawned in the Nittany Valley, new challenges and opportunities arose. Mr. Kogelmann announced he was going to timber his 213 acres—at the time, we told people he was going to clear cut, because that sounded worse.

We told him we didn't want it cut, and he said in effect, "Well fine, then buy the land." The price for Mr. Kogelmann's 213 acres was now $200,000. I did not think we could raise $200,000, so I went home the day I got that news feeling pretty defeated. But then I began thinking it through as a lawyer, and I went back to him with another proposal.

I proposed that Mr. Kogelmann sell us 120 acres for $120,000, and then donate the other 93 acres. We would form the Mount Nittany Conservancy as a nonprofit, which would mean Mr. Kogelmann would get a healthy tax deduction that would make up for that $80,000 difference. He did the computations and said, "Yes, let's do it. It's a good deal."

He offered us an option to purchase the 213 acres. We would put down $20,000 and have one year to complete the purchase by raising the remaining $100,000 and taking the option.

In 1981 I had been elected president of Lion's Paw Alumni Association, and we served for two-year terms. At my final meeting as president before I went out of office, I put this proposal to the LPAA board to commit us to this arrangement with Mr. Kogelmann. This would require us to raise the money and enter into an Agreement of Sale, or else we would lose the $20,000 we put down. This was my last meeting as president of LPAA in 1983, and new officers were elected that resulted in me setting back to work as LPAA's treasurer.

With LPAA support for the creation of the Mount Nittany Conservancy and the Kogelmann arrangement, we had a basis to go out and raise the money. I felt certain we could.

TAS: Alright, so at this point it's Homecoming 1983, and you're treasurer of Lion's Paw Alumni Association and in charge of animating the Mount Nittany Conservancy as an entirely new group for the preservation of the Mountain. What did this involve, both strategically and tactically?

BN: First, the Mount Nittany Conservancy required a way for conveying our vision for the Mountain—really an entire campaign plan for raising the $120,000 we needed to raise. And we needed to assemble a board of directors for the nonprofit corporation. This was not only required legally, but also for the purpose of appealing to the entire community with names that people would recognize and trust.

Our 1984 plan was called "The Magic of the Mountain: The Campaign to Save Mount Nittany," and this introduced both the Mount Nittany Conservancy and our vision to the community.

At the same time I began assembling our first board that would be such a critical part of making this a successful campaign.

I put together a board with folks like Bill Welch, editor of the *Centre Daily Times*; Bob Zimmerman, who owned WRSC and other radio and television stations; Mimi Coppersmith who ran a local advertising company, Joe Paterno; and several other leading personalities in the community who were eager to join.

TAS: This is really the moment, then, when Mount Nittany becomes in a sense a common endeavor, isn't it? How did you get people like Coach Paterno onto the board of a startup nonprofit?

BN: Right. Well, I could easily get great people to join because I promised them they would never have to attend a meeting!

I could achieve this perhaps rather strange-sounding feat by saying, "I'll send everything we're going to do at the meetings *before* the meeting—the exact resolutions we're going to pass. If there are any objections, let me know in advance and we'll have a meeting. Otherwise, send me back your proxy and I'll conduct the meeting by reading all the proxies, recording the decisions of the board, and moving forward very simply."

In this way, we never had to require attendance at board meetings. I sent board members everything in advance, giving them full knowledge of everything we were doing, and they would send back their proxies, so we never had to meet.

Very few people enjoy long, bureaucratic meetings. This was a way to ensure we took care of our legal responsibilities, but in a way that wouldn't be very demanding and could keep the whole endeavor efficient and fun.

So we formed the Conservancy in this way and I started the campaign and we got all these people together through the spring and summer of 1984.

TAS: All this sounds surprisingly simple for something of this scale. You had the support of LPAA for the campaign and the creation of the Mount Nittany Conservancy, you put together "The Magic of the Mountain" plan, and assembled this new board team. Was it difficult at any point getting the buy-in necessary to do these things?

BN: Well, yes. We ran into difficulties. During this period the president of LPAA who had been elected at Homecoming 1983 decided to resign in the spring of 1984. He didn't believe we could raise the money and thought we would embarrass ourselves. So he sent in his letter of resignation.

This meant that not only did we not have a president, but we had no way to elect a new one until the next meeting in the fall. The vice president was also skeptical that the money could be raised but, rather than resigning, remained incommunicado—he simply refused to answer telephone calls or letters. We were left with me as treasurer and Ross Lehman as secretary. Ross and I met for lunch and Ross says, "Ben, no one thinks we can raise the money. I sort of agree with them." Now, Ross saying this didn't bother me, because at least I could talk with him; and in any event, I knew if we raised the money it would be no problem.

It was in August 1984 that I met with Mr. Kogelmann to get the Agreement of Sale. The problem was that even though Willy agreed to it, we didn't have any officers to sign it. You had to have a president and a secretary sign it. The president had resigned and the secretary wasn't very interested at the moment.

I said to Mr. Kogelmann, "If you keep this agreement open, I'll raise the money." In other words, all we had between us was a verbal agreement and a handshake. I started "The Magic of the Mountain" campaign to raise the money. For the next four months I was terrified because we were creating all this publicity and raising all this money without anything in writing. I knew that at any time Willy could pull the rug out from under me by simply saying, "Gee, I've changed my mind." It would have been tremendously embarrassing to have to send back all the donations. But Willy stayed the course. He stayed right there with me.

TAS: This is a pretty dramatic birth for the Mount Nittany Conservancy. What led you to push forward? You were left as the lone acting officer of the board to raise $120,000 and even your Agreement of Sale was entirely on faith at this point.

BN: It might sound naïve these days, but like I've said, I really believed there was this reservoir of goodwill and spirit throughout the Nittany Valley. I was banking on it in a fairly literal way, and the people sure came through.

We raised about $100,000 by January 1985, and so Mr. Kogelmann and I got together to get that Agreement of Sale written up and signed. In the meantime I had been elected at Homecoming 1984 to fill the term of the president who had resigned. As a result, I was president of both Lion's Paw Alumni Association and the Mount Nittany Conservancy.

And so it was that finally we had officers who could sign the agreement, because I was president, and Ross Lehman was happy as secretary because we had raised the money.

At this point I met with Mr. Kogelmann for three days to hammer things out. Let me tell you, those were the most miserable three days of my life.

We had negotiations in Bob Kistler's office, who was a great guy. Willy was great too, of course, but he wanted things which I knew would get incredibly bad publicity. For instance, he wanted the right to continue to hunt on Mount Nittany for the rest of his life, and several other things, like a right-of-way.

I was just happy to say, "Fine, for the rest of your life." Willy was in his 50s at the time, and a real Type-A personality. I figured, "Ah, he'll have a heart attack before too long!"

Of course, Willy lived for nearly another thirty years—he died October 24, 2011. Let me emphasize that I was, of course, happy to see him live so long. I'm really glad he was able to enjoy the Mountain for so long, and was thrilled to see the Mount Nittany Conservancy honor him with its first-ever "Friend of the Mountain" award in 2010. He absolutely deserved it.

But every one of those three days was hard bargaining, and Willy sent me home utterly exhausted trying to hammer out a deal. Finally we got one, but I had to give in to almost everything he wanted. After all, he had all the leverage, and we both knew it.

We got the agreement, and the Mount Nittany Conservancy was able to prove there really was a "magic" about Mount Nittany. We did get some really bad publicity from the things I had to give in on. But I knew we would be alright in the long run. Most of all, what pulled me through was the simple belief that all of us are only human and will pass away, but the Mount Nittany Conservancy is forever—when Willy and I and the others are gone, Mount Nittany will still be here centuries from now.

That's really what we were working toward building, after all.

TAS: Let's step back a bit in terms of the timeline. You've raised the money for the Mount Nittany Conservancy and got the agreement settled with Mr. Kogelmann, but let's look at the specifics of the campaign itself.

It took place over the course of essentially a few red-hot months in the autumn of 1984 and winter of 1985. Where did the money come from?

BN: The support came from many people and groups. We raised about $35,000 in individual donations from people all over the area. This came in the form of small donations of $100, or usually $15 or $25, from local citizens, alumni, students, parents, and others. It was really gratifying to read the notes and letters that came in with their donations.

I want to mention with special gratitude the work of my secretary, Marsha Walker, who was in charge of recording and depositing the donations, and sending out thank-you letters. Often this reached more than a couple of hundred a week. She did this voluntarily in addition to the legal work of my law office. As a result, when the mail piled up in her office, she was often heard to mutter, "Clear-cut the Mountain." But it was all in good fun, and she still savors the memories of all we did in the campaign.

Others were critical fundraisers, including student groups, dormitory houses, fraternities, and so forth raising a few hundred here and there. We were also selling t-shirts and Mount Nittany booklets—we were doing quite a number of little things like that. Bill Welch even helped us get a "First Day Cover stamp" from the American Philatelic Society. W.R. Hickey beer distributor gave us $1 on every case of Budweiser they sold for a month. But while these all might seem like little things, they took an enormous amount of work—putting together the booklets, designing, ordering and delivering t-shirts, speaking to student groups many evenings, sending thank you notes, preparing press releases for the newspaper and radio stations on everything we did to create a constant media presence for the campaign.

A major contribution to "The Magic of the Mountain" campaign came in the form of a $25,000 check from Alan R. Wareheim, Class of 1935. Alan was a Lion's Paw alumnus and president of Hanover Foods, which had a plant in Centre County. Now, only a few years prior to this in the early 1970s, I represented residents in the area who were suing Hanover, and I even brought a criminal action against Hanover Foods naming its president. But Alan didn't hold that against me. This was a time when people understand the idea that, "Well, that's your job." I should explain that I withdrew that criminal action and we settled the case long before any dream of the Conservancy came to be—but he could have held all that against me. Thankfully people just didn't act that way back then.

Another special person who was crucial to the success of "The Magic of the Mountain" campaign was Jack Ryan, Class of 1935, another Lion's Paw alumnus. He was president of Mine Safety Appliances corporation, and had kept in touch with me from the very first time LPAA raised money to make the Lee purchase back in about 1978. Jack frequently sent checks as well as shares of stock in his company, which LPAA would then sell. When we began the Conservancy campaign, Jack also said he'd help us get a grant, and told me to apply to the Richard King Mellon Foundation, which has long supported conservation causes. That grant came through in December 1984, just before

Christmas, in the amount of $40,000. That was one of the most memorable Christmas gifts ever. Up till then, we had only raised about $60,000, and I was worried that the campaign might run out of steam. But with that grant, we went over $100,000, and I knew we could raise the rest.

TAS: Alright, so this brings us to $100,000—six figures. Impressive, but it means you've still got $20,000 to go. Can you flesh out the specifics of how you essentially single-handedly raised the initial $35,000 from within the community?

BN: Right—by 1985 we had $20,000 left to raise. Of this remaining amount more than half was raised once more from inside the Nittany Valley. And the story of the final $5,000 is a particularly beautiful moment in the history of Mount Nittany, and the early history of the Conservancy.

Do you remember old Bill Ulerich, the *Centre Daily Times* editor who called together the initial group of Lion's Paw alumni to save Mount Nittany all the way back in 1945? Well, by 1985 Bill had become an even more eminent and devoted man— former editor of the *Centre Daily Times*, a past-president of the Penn State Board of Trustees, and owner of the *Clearfield Progress* newspaper as well as a radio station. Anyway, Bill calls me up and says, "I'll give you the last $5,000 you need to put you over the top, so just let me know when you're ready."

I went into the home stretch knowing that I had Bill's unwavering commitment to Mount Nittany, and that we needed just $15,000 more—but I was also exhausted by this point.

I was going out every day to get that $35,000 from people all over the region. I would visit every group that met for breakfast, lunch, or dinner in the county—we're talking hundreds of groups, from retired federal employees to old-age homes to Rotary, Kiwanis, and Lions Clubs to religious groups. I went to every one to give a talk on Mount Nittany. Sometimes I was scheduled to speak to three or four groups every weekday for weeks on end!

I went to every public and private grade school, high school, and elementary school in county, sharing the legends and stories of Mount Nittany. The idea was that every young person in Centre County would have heard of Mount Nittany and the legends by the end of the campaign, and every older person would at least have seen the slideshow that I had put together. It was my hope that these kids would remember it, and that they would pass down something of the specialness of Mount Nittany to their kids. I liked to think that what I was doing would keep the sacredness of the Mountain alive for another century. In the back of my mind was always the idea that I was passing down the feeling for Mount Nittany that Mike Lynch had passed on to me.

We also received great support from local media like the *Centre Daily Times* and WRSC and WMAJ radio stations—from everybody except the Penn State administration, in fact.

The reason for this was that we were starting the Mount Nittany Conservancy and raising these funds at the same time Bryce Jordan and the administration was starting "The Campaign for Penn State," the first major fundraising campaign the university ever put together. They feared our campaign for Mount Nittany would conflict with theirs, so even as we were getting great publicity and as word was spreading about the Mount Nittany Conservancy and the Mountain, the bureaucracy of Penn State itself was very mum about it.

I knew people in Old Main at the time who said that the top administration didn't like it, but at that time I still had a lot of friends in Old Main who knew we had to run "The Magic of the Mountain" campaign anyway. I figured, "We'll just have to show them that it's good for Penn State spirit," which it was.

As our campaign was nearing its end and the final $15,000 was pouring in from various people and groups—including $5,000 raised from the Phi Psi 500—we were getting statements from President and Mrs. Jordan and many others in the administration who were then willing to support it.

We braved it all—we got through it, raising the money by April 1985. I called up Bill Ulerich and he put us over the top to complete the purchase.

TAS: Your methods for raising money directly from the people of the community through speaking to civic clubs, schools, and other associations reminds me of the remarkable story of the assembly of the Statue of Liberty.

While you and the Conservancy don't represent an exact parallel to Joseph Pulitzer and his *New York World* newspaper, I think the stories do reflect some similarities.

While the Statue of Liberty herself was a gift from the French, it didn't arrive in New York's harbor in the way it proudly stands today. It came over in pieces, and without a pedestal for her to stand upon. The New York City government didn't have the money to assemble Lady Liberty, so publisher Joseph Pulitzer decided to ask the people of New York directly through his newspapers for the money needed to do the job.

Pulitzer and his *New York World* appealed to the people of the city in 1885 saying:

"We must raise the money! The World is the people's paper, and now it appeals to the people to come forward and raise the money. The $250,000 that the making of the Statue cost was paid in by the masses of the French people—by the working men, the tradesmen, the shop girls, the artisans—by all, irrespective of class or condition. Let us respond in like manner. Let us not wait for the millionaires to give us this money. It is not a gift from the millionaires of France to the millionaires of America, but a gift of the whole people of France to the whole people of America."

Over the course of six months, more than 120,000 citizens contributed the money to construct the pedestal for the Statue of Liberty—and most contributions were less than a dollar.

A century later, a Pulitzer-sized broadsheet didn't exist for you in Centre County, but like him you did make it a public, common campaign and achieved success where others had not.

What were you saying to the people of the Nittany Valley to be so effective?

BN: It was my basic principle that when speaking to groups about Mount Nittany I would never ask for money. Often after giving a talk to Rotary or Kiwanis or Lion's Club, for example, I would sit down and the person next to me would nudge my arm and say, "You forgot to ask for donations." I would then point to the people coming forward with open checkbooks in their hands, and say, "That's why I don't ask for donations—they come forward on their own."

We needed the money, of course, but I felt that the important thing about the campaign was conveying that there really was a spirit of magic about Mount Nittany. If people ended up feeling some of that spirit by the end of my talk, or by the end of my letters, for instance, it usually meant that they wanted to find a way to support our work.

In general, I flouted just about all the conventional rules of fundraising. I wrote long, detailed letters about the Mountain—often more than 10 pages, single spaced—rather than short, zippy solicitation-type mailers. I wanted to convey the specialness of the Mountain and the chance for anyone to become a part of its legendary history. I was never shy about conveying as much history and love as I could in each letter.

And these long letters, they really worked. For example, a friend of my sister, who was also a friend of mine and working on Wall Street, called me one day. She told me that a lot of people at work were all talking about a long letter one of them had received about preserving a mountain, and had brought it in to show everyone in the office. So she ended up reading it, saw who signed the letter, and had called me up to ask, "Are you the same Ben Novak who wrote that letter?" Her office was buzzing about it.

Another event I recall fondly was the 1985 Lion's Paw banquet. That was the first Lion's Paw banquet that former U.S. Senator Richard Schweiker attended, as far as I recall. As soon as

I walked in, he came over to me and said, "This is the first LP banquet I've been to in years, and I only came because I wanted to meet the guy who writes those letters about Mount Nittany."

This meant a great deal to me, because I had read a great deal about him in *The Daily Collegians* of the late 1940s, when he was one of the most outstanding student leaders at Penn State. Senator Schweiker, you may recall, was selected by Ronald Reagan to be his vice presidential running mate at the 1976 Republican convention. Unfortunately, Reagan wasn't nominated that time, but Richard Schweiker had been a student leader hero of mine long before that.

As far as specific examples of what we were saying during the campaign, I'll point to the following advertisement we place in the *Centre Daily Times* during the autumn of 1984, which while considerably shorter than my letters, conveys the same spirit:

A Mountain Needs Your Support

The beauty of Mount Nittany can be forever—if we act to preserve it today.

Mount Nittany is once again threatened by the woodsman's axe.

Almost 40 years ago loggers threatened to cut the whole top of The Mountain. A few alumni banded together to save it. They formed the Lion's Paw Alumni Association and raised the money to purchase more than 500 acres.

Now a neighboring parcel containing over 200 acres is threatened with clear-cutting. This parcel is situated between the Lion's Paw and Rockview lands. It faces the new State College By-pass and Route 322, extending to the summit of the Mountain. It will be the first thing to be seen by every visitor coming to The University on Route 322. The owner has agreed to donate one tract containing about 89 acres if the money can be raised to purchase the second tract containing 120 acres at $1,000 per acre.

This time a new organization has been formed to help meet the threat to the Mountain. It is The Mount Nittany Conservancy, Inc. The Conservancy was created as an independent non-profit corporation, separate from the University, in 1981 to help involve members of the Centre Region, the Penn State community, and alumni in preserving the beauty and the legend of Mount Nittany.

Now is the time to act. The Conservancy must raise $120,000 to purchase the land. To assure that the support is there to complete the purchase, your contribution and pledge is needed today. Your support will decide whether Mount Nittany is preserved or is developed.

Mount Nittany is Penn State's most important symbol and the legendary home of the Nittany Lion. It is also the most beautiful natural landmark of the Nittany Valley, overlooking all of the villages and municipalities of the Centre Region. Visitors know it as the symbol of our Alma Mater and our community.

To preserve the Mountain for future generations is the prime goal of the Mount Nittany Conservancy.

It is not often that a Mountain needs your support. Today one does. If Mount Nittany is to be preserved from having more than 200 acres of her trees cut, and the Mountain land sold off for subdivision and development, your help is needed today.

The Mount Nittany Conservancy, Inc. has been recognized as tax exempt by the Internal Revenue Service. All contributions are tax deductible.

Princess Nit-A-Nee and the Lion will appreciate your help to save their legendary home. Please paw through your checkbook and send your contribution today to The Mount Nittany Conservancy, Inc., P.O. Box 10, Lemont, PA, 16851-0010.

TAS: One of the things the Mount Nittany Conservancy is known for today is its offering of "Life Estate Deeds." These are square-inches of Mount Nittany that the Conservancy sells, and the Deeds themselves are really heirloom-quality gifts. You were behind this concept, weren't you?

BN: Yes. The Life Estate Deeds were an idea I had from my childhood. When I was about 9 years old in Johnstown I saw an offer on the back of my morning cereal box from a group selling square-inches of land in Alaska. I still have three or four of those Alaskan square-inch deeds somewhere.

As we were running "The Magic of the Mountain" campaign, I had beautiful deeds designed with the idea to sell square-inches of Mount Nittany. We got a particular plot of our land surveyed —about 20'x20', which gave us 57,600 square inches. This legal arrangement was approved by Centre County Planning Commission, and we had it recorded in the Office of Recorder of Deeds, which means that when you buy a Life Estate Deed from the Mount Nittany Conservancy, you're buying a real deed to a real piece of land on the Mountain.

We wanted to make sure the Life Estate Deeds were really something special, so at the time I went and got special vellum paper, and tracked down the last engraver in Pennsylvania.

Everybody used to have engraved stationary, where the engraving was achieved with a special piece of metal used to raise the paper, resulting in a beautiful embossed seal. With computerization, you can now do it with plastic incredibly cheaply, and so engraved stationary is a thing of the past. Well, we got Pennsylvania's last engraver to engrave our initial Life Estate Deeds. That means that the initial 1,000 or so deeds we printed and sold are really collectors items for that reason alone. The deeds today do not have that engraving, but for those who have some of those original deeds, they possess a real work of art.

In fact, the engraving our man did for the Mount Nittany Conservancy was the last engraving he performed, so those first deeds are rather unusual in that respect as well.

TAS: You presented one of the Mount Nittany Conservancy's Life Estate Deeds to The Nittany Valley Society in December 2012. It was our first community gathering, and took place in the

Beaver Room at the Hotel State College. It was really a special day, and your gift of the Life Estate Deed played a special part.

BN: It was a lovely day, indeed. You know I'm thrilled to see what Chris Buchignani and so many others are building with The Nittany Valley Society, and it was a pleasure to speak that day about the two books of mine that The Nittany Valley Society has published: *Is Penn State a Real University: An Investigation of the University as a Living Ideal* and *The Birth of the Craft Brew Revolution*. The craft brew beer tasting downstairs at Zeno's certainly didn't hurt as a way to end the day, either.

If the Life Estate Deed was well received, that's exactly the point, and the Mount Nittany Conservancy sells dozens of them every year to supporters. As an example of the language of the deed itself, the following is how The Nittany Valley Society's Life Estate Deed reads:

> *This Deed, dated the 1st day of December A.D. 2012, for good and valuable consideration, grants and conveys legal title to a Life Estate in a tract or parcel of land on the famed Mount Nittany to The Nittany Valley Society, Grantee(s).*
>
> *The Mount Nittany Conservancy, Inc., Grantor herein, grants and conveys to the said Grantee(s), a tract or parcel of land One (1) square inch in size, and being designated as parcel No. 008-190 on a plot or plan recorded in the Office of the Recorder of Deeds of Centre County, Pennsylvania in Plot Book Vol. 34, at page 28, subject to all easements, covenants and restrictions of record.*

Being a portion of the same premises which Mathilda Boal Lee and Blair Lee III, her husband, by deed dated May 10, 1985, and recorded in the Office of the Recorder of Deeds of Centre County, at Deed Book Vol. 431, at page 1015, granted and conveyed to The Mount Nittany Conservancy, Inc., Grantor herein.

The Mount Nittany Conservancy, Inc., specially warrants and will forever defend this deed conveying to the said Grantee(s), for the term of his, her, or their natural life or lives, an ownership interest in a piece of the famed Mount Nittany, legendary lair of the Nittany Lion and legendary Burial Mound of the mysterious Indian Princess and the Indian Brave she loved.

May Mount Nittany stand forever as the Guardian before the Gates of Old Penn State, our breaker against the harsh winds of destiny and fate, source of fearless courage and deathless love, both father and mother of the games by which we live, and guarantee of the life of the Valley we love.

The undersigned have been duly authorized by Resolution of the Board of Directors of The Mount Nittany Conservancy, Inc., to execute and deliver this Life Estate Deed to the Grantee(s) herein, who, by these presents, for the rest of his, her, or their natural life or lives, shall own a piece of the famed Mount Nittany, and shall become a part of the Legend.

Attest, The Mount Nittany Conservancy, Inc.
Douglas A. Wion   *John Hook*
Secretary   *President*

By the way, the parcel number of the specific square inch conveyed to you (008-190) refers to its location in the surveyed 20'x20' subdivision. Since 20' is 240 inches, the first number 008 refers to the eighth column of 240 inches, and yours is the 190th square inch from the top. So, your deed is for the 1,870th sold (7x240+190). When we first thought of the 20'x20' plot, we planned for enough square inches to be sold to last a century. After your deed, there are still 55,730 more square inches available.

TAS: The Mount Nittany Conservancy's campaign was a success, both in the sense that "The Magic of the Mountain" raised the money to preserve Mr. Kogelmann's 213 acres—not to mention its later acquisitions—and also in the sense that the Conservancy itself has become a fixture of the local community. Each time I return to the Nittany Valley I can't help but marvel at its physical beauty, but I also marvel at the fact that I can't even open a menu at The Corner Room without seeing a blurb for the work of the Mount Nittany Conservancy.

What are your thoughts nearly 30 years after the initial campaign? Is the Mount Nittany Conservancy where you imagined it would be?

BN: First, I'm extremely happy the Conservancy has thrived so tremendously and continues to bring in top members of the community, hosting social and community functions and preserving the Mountain in all sorts of ways. It's exactly what we dreamed that it would be.

The present officers and board members and volunteers are exactly what was envisioned and hoped for. Mount Nittany is so obviously well taken care of—all you need to do is hike it to see what I mean—and in recent years things like Mount Nittany Night, the "Friend of the Mountain" tradition, the Mount Nittany Marathon, and the continuing ties with students are wonderful things.

I should note that after starting the Conservancy off on its path, getting it incorporated, recognized as a nonprofit, and raising those funds, I did not stay involved with the effort. This is due to fundamental differences in philosophy and approach between me and the subsequent officers.

What I mean is this: I started the Mount Nittany Conservancy when nobody believed we could raise the money. I went against the leadership of my organization and the university administration and many people in town who thought it was a fool's errand. I was banking completely on the emotional attachment of alumni, students, and townspeople to preserving the sacredness of the Mountain and preserving it in its natural state. I bet everything on that, and the alumni, townspeople, and students came through.

But my approach to fundraising was totally different from the normal approach. As I was traveling across the county giving my talks, so many told me, "This is not how *anyone* raises money." But I said, "Well, we're going to do it differently here, because we've got something special."

The contemporary ways of raising money that work normally essentially involve contacting wealthy people and getting their support, whereas I was going out to the general public and had to create a public relations campaign—these are totally different approaches.

Let me explain how these two approaches intertwine. Although we have so far talked of raising $120,000, because that's what we needed to buy the land, we actually had to raise a total of about $140,000, because we had about $20,000 in expenses. We had to pay for advertisements in the Centre Daily Times and radio stations, printing for booklets and posters, paying the engraver and for the printing of the deeds on vellum, and a huge postage cost for all our mailings. Of that total sum of $140,000, about $75,000 came from major donors (Mellon Foundation, Jack Ryan, Alan Wareheim, and Bill Ulerich), leaving more than $65,000 from small donations. But it was the small donations that had to come in first, in order to get the larger donors to take us seriously. Usually, in normal fundraising campaigns like "The Campaign for Penn State," the big donations are already in place before the campaign is announced. That's why professional fundraising campaigns are always successful. I had to start with no assurance of large donations or success—only after we had shown that the public strongly supported us with small donations did the large donors commit. So, I had to run an entirely different kind of fundraising campaign, which had to build on something that had never been tested, which was my (and Mike Lynch's) belief that there really was a "magic of the Mountain."

Thus, when new officers came in with their modern approach I was very happy that they were going to be able to bring things back within the normal ways of fundraising and running an organization. This meant stability for the future in a way that depended less on "magic," "sacredness," "historical-mythical" ideas, or particular personalities.

When the new officers came in by the late 1980s, I said in effect, "You take it over and run it the modern way, because that's what we need now." What I did was not what would likely work after our initial success—but without that initial approach it seems likely that we never would have even gotten the Mount Nittany Conservancy off the ground.

So I've been extremely happy with the officers and conduct of the Mount Nittany Conservancy, even as I've stayed on the sidelines watching it unfold—although I have attended an occasional meeting, and do attend certain Lion's Paw gatherings.

It's my hope that even as the future unfolds, the original idea of Lion's Paw stays with those who work to preserve the Mountain—the idea of preserving it in its natural state.

We've talked about the various efforts to prevent logging on the Mountain. Every single forester in the world will tell you that if you want to preserve that kind of land, you should do selective cutting every few years to allow for different growths. But from the beginning we've sort of rejected the modern scientific principles in favor of just letting it grow on its own—leaving it like the Indians left it.

This is part of what makes the Mount Nittany Conservancy unique, and I'm glad we're doing things our own way. We now have more than a century of growth on the Mountain since it was clear-cut in the early 20th century. In other words, after a century without cutting, it's back as much as it can get to its natural state. There's a danger of forest fire when you let it grow like that, so we pray to God every year that we don't get a forest fire—but it's in its natural state the way the Indians left it, the way we found it, and that's the way we want to leave it to the next generation.

TAS: I'm not sure that among Penn State freshmen today, for instance, that there's this historical-mythical sort of feeling for Mount Nittany that seems to have so profoundly characterized it generation after generation. At least from an environmental perspective I think there's certainly a consciousness of the importance of the Mountain. Do you see a pull between these two poles—between the sacred and legendary versus the ecological and environmental? Can the Mount Nittany Conservancy continue to tell the story of the Mountain in a compelling way that speaks to both aspects of the conservationist impulse?

BN: I'll tell you a story that might serve as an answer to your questions. In late 1984 when we were just starting our public campaign, I contacted The Nature Conservancy. The Nature Conservancy sent a biologist down from Boston to see if there were any rare fauna or flora on the Mountain that would make it of interest to them for preservation, and he arrived in town early one Sunday morning.

We went up together on Mount Nittany, and he looked all over as we tromped around the Mountain. As we were walking down, I asked him, "What do you think?" And he responded by saying, "Well, I'm going to recommend that we help you preserve this mountain." I was delighted to hear it, and asked him why. His response was perfect:

"I haven't been able to find any unique fauna or flora. In fact, there's nothing unique to this mountain whatsoever. It's not an exceptional mountain in any way. *But*, we ought to preserve at least one of these ordinary mountains! Nobody else is likely to do it. So, I'll recommend it on that basis—that we're preserving just an ordinary Pennsylvania hill."

You see, even as late as the 1980s, there was nothing about Mount Nittany that environmentalists were particularly interested in—except its sheer ordinariness. And, by the way, we never again heard from The Nature Conservancy. So, it was purely the "historical-mythical" dimension, as you say—the sacredness and legendary aspects—that motivated people to preserve the Mountain.

This was the historical situation. At first there was nothing about Mount Nittany worth protecting environmentally, because there were lots of virgin forests all around State College and throughout Central Pennsylvania. But it was sacred to us, as the people of this valley, from the beginning, so that's what mattered and that's why it was conserved. Its sacred aura and spirit, its myths and legends, its function as a symbol, its source of history and stories and camaraderie. These are the things that made it worthy of preservation, even if an environmentalist could only recommend preserving it among fellow experts as an example of the ordinary.

We talk about ecological and environmental concerns today because they have become more important than they once were. When virgin territory was everywhere around us, we took it for granted. But Mount Nittany has now become completely surrounded by development that has filled the valleys, so it is now environmentally justified—the idea of preserving the Mountain as open space in its natural state.

In other words, today I think both aspects play a role. The historical-mythical aspect continues to play the central role, however, because it explains why we chose to save *this specific Mountain*, rather than any other piece of land. Learning the story tells you something about it, and I think knowing about the place is the only reason you would care to think about it environmentally.

When you have an emotional or spiritual attachment to something, it's much easier to preserve it. Tapping into these feelings has been vital to the continuing work of the Mount Nittany Conservancy, and it's what has allowed us to appeal so successfully to the entire Nittany Valley community.

III.
Mount Nittany
Today and Tomorrow

The story of Mount Nittany is the story of a people. We have explored the basis for the people of the Nittany Valley's extraordinary response to an ordinary Pennsylvania hill. We have learned about Mount Nittany's role in the history of Penn State and the region, and about the efforts of Lion's Paw alumni and, in time, an entire community working through the Mount Nittany Conservancy, to conserve and convey the Mountain as a gift for the future. This chapter will serve as our final conversation with Dr. Novak, and represents a closing meditation on the meaning of the Mountain as we lean in to the future.

The Nittany Valley has many customs and traditions, many things that an entire people can share. Ours are not simply common experiences in the sense that mere group participation makes them special. In other words, they are not merely programs, in the way we might put together an entertainment or vacation experience. While specific customs change with the fashions and interests of the time, *traditions* stand apart as chances to encounter eternity because they are opportunities to live in the spirit of those who have come before us.

In the best sense, the Nittany Valley is a traditional place, and Mount Nittany is an example of one of our traditions.

Even eras that prize novelty over tradition seem to recognize its worth. This is one reason the traditional camaraderie, pageantry, and community feeling of America's college towns still strike us as special—and maybe even magical—in our own time.

There's a subtle force at work in the carrying on of tradition, in the act of commemorating timeless treasures of people and places. Authentic traditions transform their participants. Traditions are encounters with a particular way of living, and no real community can exist without a particular, common way of life. Not everyone is comfortable with living in the spirit of any given place, and so traditions are a gentle, beautiful way of both cultivating and conveying a community's spirit.

In responding to the traditions of the Nittany Valley, we tell the story of our time. At any point we could choose to neglect the tradition of affection and conservation of Mount Nittany. We *choose* to carry it on, and in so doing we choose to add a few more pages to the story of the Nittany Valley that cohere with our past —with Henry W. Shoemaker, with Fred Lewis Pattee, with Bill Ulerich and Russell Clark and Ridge Riley, with Lion's Paw and the Mount Nittany Conservancy.

Like the American Indian legends that tell of Nit-A-Nee's "deathless love," for her people in the valley, we're writing our own love story in the way we treat and pass along the spirit of the Nittany Valley for its Mountain.

The purpose of a parable is to convey truth in story form. The Nit-A-Nee legends and even the early history of Mount Nittany's preservation, though we know it in fact occurred, are parables about our nature—and they are also parables about our tradition. They convey the truth of our Nittany Valley story—about how a people can live with a common spirit.

Mount Nittany helps bind us together as both an object of our admiration and affection, and as a symbol of our spirit. It is a tradition of ours in our immemorial valley.

Speaking at Penn State's IFC/Panhellenic Dance Marathon on February 16, 2013, Jay Paterno addressed students in the midst of another great Nittany Valley tradition.

"This morning, as I do most Saturdays," Paterno said, "I went and visited my dad. His grave is on a hillside and you can see Mount Nittany. Mount Nittany to me is a symbol of eternity. It's there, it was there before any of us, and will be there long after us."

If we can learn to live in the spirit of Mount Nittany, and of those things that have been present "before any of us," we'll be entering the pages of a love story that will be told long after us.

We might even discover that a small part of ourselves has found a way to live forever, in the valley we love.

TAS: Mount Nittany is a beautiful thing, and the efforts to conserve the Mountain over the years are a powerful example of a community working together. Yet I'm left wondering—even with the Mount Nittany Conservancy appealing to the community as a whole—whether Mount Nittany might in some ways simply be a special interest.

The Centre Foundation, for instance, which is Centre County's community foundation, lists some 250 distinct funds to which interested donors can contribute. Each fund is endowed for some special purpose in building up and sustaining the community, benefitting local interests ranging from the Nittany Valley Symphony to schoolchildren's scholarships. In 1999, thanks to a gift from Tom Smyth and others, the Mount Nittany Conservancy has had an endowment of its own that helps it cover its operational costs.

Where does the Mount Nittany Conservancy and its mission fit in to the contemporary community? Is Mount Nittany simply one symbolic, special interest among many?

BN: I think that Mount Nittany pulls this area together. It's common today for many to think of the Mountain for its environmental values—open space, for recreation and enjoyment, for example. But if the lands held by Lion's Law and the Mount Nittany Conservancy were ever sold or subdivided for development, a lot more would be lost than simply open space and recreation space. Rather, it would make a lot of people feel that something very special to our souls—something kind of sacred—had been lost to the area.

The Conservancy has got to have a way to pay its basic costs of operating. The Centre Foundation endowment is undoubtedly important, but Mount Nittany is more than the Conservancy, and it's more than any single person or group can add to it.

We can all enjoy Mount Nittany in an obvious and personal way for hiking, getting back to nature, or simply enjoying the view. So, for all those who enjoy the Mountain in this way it's personal, and in that sense they have a special interest in it. Yet Mount Nittany is more than just an environmental resource—it's a common symbol of who we are. Hike the Mountain and you'll understand what I mean. It's always there, waiting for you.

In this way I think of Mount Nittany as something sacred, and in the context of conservation, a sacred duty both for its own sake and for one another.

TAS: Where does this attitude come from? What I'd like to better understand is this: As our community grows, how can this common feeling for the Mountain avoid being crowded out? Where did Mike Lynch pick it up his love for the Mountain, for instance? It seems like he was absolutely one to think about the Mountain as a sacred duty.

BN: I believe that at certain points in history people find themselves sitting around and looking for meaningful things. It often turns out that these moments are inflection points in the unfolding story of a place.

For Mount Nittany, that moment began right alongside the development of the early Penn State spirit and tradition. You had students and professors thinking and speaking about Mount Nittany, conducting rituals, sharing hiking and camping experiences, and all sorts of things. Over time so many had shared such experiences that a common feeling ran through the entire community.

We were becoming the Nittany Lions, and with Mount Nittany being the legendary home of the Lion, it just entered into our consciousness that the Mountain was a special thing.

When that *Centre Daily Times* notice appeared in 1945 offering to sell Mount Nittany for logging, you had Russell Clark and others ready to act immediately to preserve it because it had already become a part of their psyches. They felt a need to protect it as something that was a special and meaningful thing.

Where does this feeling for Mount Nittany, or protecting meaningful things in general, come from?

I think the context for these feelings is simply *community*. The Lion's Paw actions, for instance, were simply a case of a group of men who were a part of a special community, and when you belong to something it's natural to feel a desire to protect it. Well, Mount Nittany was something that "belonged" to Penn Staters even before Lion's Paw bought those 525 acres, because they first came to admire and love the Mountain. Their love was able to spread throughout a growing community.

Of course, Lion's Paw members weren't the only ones who felt "Mount Nittany is special." The Mount Nittany Conservancy exists because a whole town, campus, and alumni community has come to feel this way, and so feel it's worth protecting forever.

TAS: You're saying, in other words, that feelings for Mount Nittany could develop, come to be shared across time, and result in groups like the Conservancy because the Nittany Valley is home to a special or distinct community?

BN: In essence, yes, but the larger point isn't that I think the Nittany Valley is special. Rather, I'm trying to convey what I mean in talking about the "context of community."

When you have a true community it isn't simply a collection of various interests and it's not simply a grouping of ages, beliefs, ethnicities, and so forth. It is first and foremost a *people*. Whatever demographic datum a social scientist might assign is less relevant than the ability for the people of a place to have genuine relationships with one another, to be able to pass word throughout the town, and to be able to know their neighbors.

This is what communities were in the old days, and you didn't need or have time for modern technological social media because there weren't as many physical or metaphorical walls to break down. You knew your neighbors and you could drop in on them for dinner. It wasn't seen as rude or imposing, even when it was unexpected or might have been rather inconvenient. It was natural when living close together to be *close*, together. If you wanted to speak to a professor, you simply called him up or swung by his office. We didn't have to call, send emails, or have secretaries scheduling everything weeks in advance. The local businesses were all owned locally—they weren't owned by chains. The owners of the banks, newspapers, drugstores, clothing stores, cafes, and restaurants often met for breakfast at the same places. This is what old folks like me mean when we say that life was less complicated before modern technology. We just mean that it didn't seem as if you had to work as hard to be together.

So this is what community once was. You knew your neighbors. You might not love every one of them, but because of so many common relationships it was natural to have common feelings about things—about Mount Nittany, in this case. It's natural for people who know each other to want to do beautiful things for each another. It's why a husband picks up flowers on the way home for his wife, or why you'll present your friend with a fine cigar or bottle of whiskey to mark a special occasion.

Conversely it is why Beaver Canyon apartment dwellers who are just anonymous students behind blank cinderblock don't care about offending their neighbors with loud music, hallway garbage, and so forth. No one has a common space to share, so no one much cares about meeting one another—so being good to one another becomes irrelevant. Not only are so many of the buildings ugly, but the attitudes and spirit they give rise to tend to be ugly, too.

When the Nittany Valley was smaller and life was less cosmopolitan, it was easy for good feelings to pass. So when money was needed for Mount Nittany, you could call up the bank president in the morning, and have a check in your hand that afternoon—you didn't need to wait weeks while the area manager contacted a regional manager who eventually got permission from the New York headquarters. Locality in a physical sense matters.

The Nittany Valley is growing and changing, but that doesn't mean community has to be lost, or that the feelings of the community for beautiful things like Mount Nittany will naturally dissipate.

New Yorkers shares symbols like the Statue of Liberty, the World Trade Center, and Central Park. They're physical realities, but they're also symbolic of the spirit of the community. Mount Nittany will be our symbol no matter how large our Nittany Valley community becomes. But like New Yorkers have, we've got to work to keep conveying the spirit for our symbols to all the new people who arrive.

This is what conserving Mount Nittany has been about in terms of the community. It's why it's been described as "public property privately owned." It's why Lion's Paw and the Mount Nittany Conservancy makes such little fuss or pretension about their ownership of the Mountain—because we know we're just passing through. We know others will be here, and more will come. We've got to have something beautiful to pass along to them—we've got to be able to do something beautiful for one another.

TAS: Your central point about knowing your neighbors and passing along common feelings is well taken. Mount Nittany and its inter-generational conservation is certainly a beautiful thing.

As you explain it, I understand what you mean about older people's sense of the "good old days." Even as it's generally more difficult to do things locally like dropping in unscheduled on someone or getting that check from the bank president after a single conversation, it's conversely now easier to try to convey a feeling or spirit broadly across a geographically dispersed community. It's simpler and cheaper to reach 10,000 like-minded people online than it is via physical mailings, as one example.

Conserving the Mountain has been such a tremendously successful, common endeavor that I'm left wondering: Is the Mount Nittany Conservancy's work done?

BN: The work of the Mount Nittany Conservancy needs to be taken up anew by every generation of students, townspeople and alumni. While we've preserved much of the Mountain, not only is there more we could purchase if new campaigns were to be undertaken, but there's always work to be done, as I think of it, in perpetuating the magic. Just as I think a real community has to be a place where you really know your neighbors, I think a real feeling for the Mountain has to be something personally communicated. Of course, it is best when it is informed by real, physical experiences on the Mountain.

In the Foreword you wrote to my book "Is Penn State a Real University?" you quoted the historian David McCullough, and his insight is so great that I hope you'll forgive me for borrowing it here. "You can't love some*thing* you don't know" McCullough says, "anymore than you can love some*one* you don't know." Well, this states it perfectly both in terms of understanding the community's duty to get to know one another, and in terms of getting to know Mount Nittany as something we all share.

As for my more personal views, my dreams for the Mount Nittany Conservancy grew as so many people responded to our campaign for the Mountain. First, we could have bought a lot more land around the Mountain—much further down so you wouldn't see houses in Lemont going up so high. This would have kept Mount Nittany as even more of a monument in the area.

Some of this is lost opportunity, but there are still many parcels of land we could add to what is already preserved.

I dreamed, secondly, of having a statue of Princess Nit-A-Nee located in the grassy area at the "Y" of the Benner Pike in front of Nittany Mall and at other places. I dreamed of having Princess Nit-A-Nee become a legendary presence to us as the personification of Mount Nittany. It just seems to me that a great Mountain ought to have a great Princess to become a symbol in the community, and the legends about her become a part of the local lore. Wouldn't it be great to have aspects of the Nittany Valley legends physically spring up as statues and monuments to our area's pre-settler heritage?

When new people and visitors entered the Nittany Valley, I imagined, they would simply look around at these things located throughout the area, and exclaim, *"Wow! Look at the spirit this place has. Look at the things they care about. Look at the history here."* They would come into the valley and feel the spirit we feel because they would see these monuments to our feeling of spirit. I think people really turn on to a place that is more than simply so many economic resources.

TAS: Leaving aside the idea of acquiring new lands on or around the Mountain, how can a person work to conserve Mount Nittany when so much of the most visible land is already safe?

BN: The conservation of Mount Nittany lies in the hearts of the Nittany Valley people. It's why it meant so much for me when we had "The Magic of the Mountain" campaign to go out and talk to just about every group in the area. By telling them about Mount Nittany I hoped to share something they would remember for the rest of their lives and pass on to their children and to every new student who came here to study. I hoped that their experience of the feelings I sought to convey would fuse with their experience of the physical landscape.

The important thing, then, is that we consider Mount Nittany as a part of our lives. This might be the most basic and important way to think about "conserving Mount Nittany" in the future. In other words, the specific ways we work to protect the Mountain are simply expressions of the feeling that lies in our hearts. The feeling is the core thing—it's what makes us decide to volunteer on the Mountain, to help maintain the trails, or prevent erosion, to tell the legends, or give talks about what Mount Nittany means to us, or raise money to purchase more land, or simply to speak about the Mountain in a reverential way.

As people continue doing all the great things necessary to protect the Mountain, people will see their great work and say, "Whoa. This isn't just some eco-action project, or just another park or recreation area. There's something else going on here." Hopefully this curiosity will lead to learning the history of the Mountain and becoming a part of the next generation of conservation.

TAS: Is it possible to talk about conserving Mount Nittany when we're physically distant from it? How many hundreds of thousands of alumni never really return to visit State College? What about the Penn State World Campus students and alumni who might never set foot in the Nittany Valley? What can

Mount Nittany be for them if it can't be experienced physically? If it can't be hiked?

BN: Everyone need symbols. Penn State administrators spent a fortune to develop the University symbol that's used today—the "1855" Nittany Lion shield that's placed on everything. Well, Mount Nittany is a symbol that's always been here and costs us nothing. We understand everything in terms of "branding" today, and so I think Mount Nittany is the perfect "brand" symbol for the spirit of the Nittany Valley and our wider community.

Even if you attend the Penn State World Campus and live far away and never set foot in the Nittany Valley, you can still choose to identify with the things we love. Mount Nittany is a beautiful thing even if we're not busy tramping around on it. Learn to carry it in your heart just like so many who live locally do. Learn to "do as the Romans do," even if you never make it to Rome.

TAS: You have lived in the Nittany Valley much of your life, but you've also spent many years far away. What is a hike up Mount Nittany for you? What are the things you carry "in your heart" when you're far away?

BN: A hike up Mount Nittany is a chance to go up and listen to the wind in the trees, and I think of that wind in the trees as the Gitchie Manitou speaking—the voice of the spirit of the place.

When I first used to walk up on the Mountain, partly because it hadn't been logged in so long, and partly because it wasn't maintained quite as diligently as it is presently, I was amazed at the experience. The trees grew so high that their leaves formed a canopy overhead, keeping the sunlight out and preventing the underbrush from growing up. Thus the trunks of the trees seemed to stand out amidst the falling leaves like pillars of a temple, and the already-fallen leaves seemed like a velvet carpet under my feet. Walking up there was like walking through a grand cathedral or a wonderful palace that for a single morning was all your own. This is what I think of when I'm far away.

Mount Nittany's magnificence is not so different even now as the Mall on campus was before the Elms began to die. You can see how magnificent the Mall was in Bill Coleman's famous "Cathedral of Elms" photograph that can be found around town.

As the Mall is like a grand and grassy avenue onto campus, Mount Nittany is like a grand and natural palace above the valley.

TAS: In E.B. White's *Here is New York* he speaks about a similar feeling. White describes an experience of Central Park on a hot night in midsummer: "In the trees the night wind stirs, bringing the leaves to life, endowing them with speech; the electric lights illuminate the green branches from the under side, translating them into a new language."

This sense of the wind bringing the leaves to life and endowing them with speech—this is something like what you have felt on Mount Nittany?

BN: Yes, that is perfect. I think of it in terms of the legends of Princess Nittany, and of Penn's Cave's "Stream of Never-Ending Love, and Grandfather Pine. One of the legends that appears in the book *The Legends of the Nittany Valley* tells the story of the formation of Penn's cave out of the Earth's love for the planet Venus, and also tells of the time the Indian Braves climbed the Grandfather Pine.

The latter legend tells of a time, as the settlers were expanding into Pennsylvania, when a meeting was called of all the American Indian tribes. All of their chiefs, medicine men, and top Braves were to meet in conclave to decide on what the response to the settlers would be. As the story tells it, they met at the Grandfather Pine, an enormous pine tree 276 feet tall. When all were assembled, they listened to the wind whispering through the limbs of the trees, and heard the Gitchie Manitou, or Great Spirit, rustling the pine's branches. The Great Spirit was calling them to climb Grandfather Pine. In response to this call they climbed the tree to meet the Great Spirit in the heavens, and they have never returned. They never came back down. As legend has it, they're still up there in the heavens with the Great Spirit, looking down on how we're taking care of the lands they knew so well. According to legend, the stars we see in the night sky are really the heavenly campfires of those American Indians who climbed Grandfather Pine.

So for me, hearing the wind in the trees is like hearing the Gitchie Manitou speaking to me just as he did to the Indians. I hear the wind, and look up through the trees in the night sky to see the stars shining like the campfires of all those chiefs and medicine men and warriors now residing in the heavens.

This is what an experience of Mount Nittany is like for me.

TAS: This is a very romantic vision. If someone's encountering all this for the first time and they're modern, practical, and not particularly given to this sort of romance, then what? What other way might you convey Mount Nittany?

BN: I know. I understand that we're not as open to such romance right now as we once were. This is why I suggest that students, or whomever, should gather to learn our legends—and that they turn the lights out in the dorms and light candles when they do it. It's the kind of thing that they will remember. It's the kind of thing that sinks down into your soul even though—or perhaps especially because—it has no practical use. It's just something special in your life—something extra that you did not bargain for; in other words, it's a magic moment.

Everyone in America wants to know, "Well, what can I do with this speaking practically?" And I respond saying, "No! *No.* You simply give someone a magic moment. A magic vision."

Why do we love the story of Harry Potter and Hogwarts and J.K. Rowling's wizarding universe, or C.S. Lewis's Narnia, or J.R.R. Tolkien's Middle Earth? It is all *magical*, and it turns out that it does us some practical good to have some magic in our lives. So I would resist the attempt to boil down how I feel about Mount Nittany into anything that might turn into a trite slogan.

I want there to be Harry Potters in Centre County. We don't have to go to England or even a theme park to experience something magical. We have such a place right in the Nittany Valley, right where we live.

TAS: One of the things the Mount Nittany Conservancy does an excellent job with is maintaining hiking paths across the

Mountain. Coupled with marketing efforts across the region, are you concerned about the risk to dilute the natural experience of the Mountain? What about problems that come with greater numbers of visitors like erosion?

BN: In 2000 I left the Nittany Valley and moved to Bratislava, Slovakia. One of the things that crushed me during my eight years in Europe was that so much of the world had become globalized.

What I mean is that many of the historic palaces, castles, and villages had become completely oriented to tourists. The paths and steps and signs that are set up for tourists end up having the effect of becoming a central part of what you're experiencing. It becomes very difficult to feel as if you're really walking on the same steps that a Medieval knight walked on, for instance. It's as though they put a wall of glass or transparent plastic between you and all the things you came to see and touch. Imagine that you lived in a world where the only way you could ever see people fall in love is in the movies.

Too much marketing and tourism-minded positioning and too many "improvements" can seriously take away from the thing you're trying to promote. Too many changes can remove the naturalness of the experience.

There's always a risk of this with Mount Nittany, but so long as there's a feeling for conserving the Mountain "as is" rather than constantly wondering what might be added to make it even better, things will be alright. Remember, the goal of Lion's Paw and the Mount Nittany Conservancy has always been to preserve Mount Nittany "in its natural state."

I think we should view Mount Nittany like Central Park in Manhattan. We want people to go and visit and enjoy. At some point we might have to do things like put in brick steps in places to ease problems like erosion, but in general you don't set out to try to improve Central Park. You just let it be, and people will keep coming because it's the one place that's just been left as-is.

TAS: Can we talk for a minute on this notion of spirit? We've talked on it throughout our conversations, but I think it remains a point of uncertainty in some ways.

Can you elaborate on what the "magic" and "spirit" of the valley are? What reality are the words trying to describe?

BN: To the ancient Greeks and Romans, as well as to the Native Americans, spirit was not something strange or difficult to grasp. They knew instinctively that nothing worthwhile could be done without spirit. They developed a multitude of ceremonies and rituals to invoke that spirit. We all know and celebrate this fact at every football game, with all sorts of pep rallies, cheerleaders, and special ways to show our spirit. It's the most concrete fact known to every coach—you can't win anything without real spirit!

Similarly, the Christian scriptures tell us that the spirit dwelt among men and that it became flesh. This is what Christians believe about Jesus Christ—that the divine spirit was incarnated in human form, and that we share in divinity by identifying with it and living in accordance with it. Whether we're telling the Christian story, building up for a football game, describing the Tao, practicing meditation, or simply telling ghost stories, the idea is always the same: a spirit can only act if it becomes, in some way, incarnate in us—that is, if people choose to live in accordance with the spirit that dwells among them. It comes into our minds and bodies and makes us come alive in a new way, and the immaterial takes on material form in our flesh and bone.

The American Indians certainly felt a spirit among them here in the Nittany Valley. We've spoken of it in our conversations, but just speaking about it isn't much more than romanticism. To encounter it you've got to climb Mount Nittany, although even then you might not feel it if you aren't open to it.

This is the paradox of spirit—that it is this invisible, intangible force and yet when someone chooses to pick it up, when it's incarnated in people by their love and tenderness and obvious sense of stewardship, then this invisible and intangible force produces visible and tangible results.

Whatever the spirit of Mount Nittany or the specialness of the Nittany Valley may be, these things as mere words probably are just romantic ideas. Our Mountain and town won't stay special unless people choose acts of conservation in their own lives. In choosing to be conservators they'll each be writing a completely new chapter in the same continuing story of Mount Nittany. They'll be responding to carrying on a tradition of the Nittany Valley, but their own chapter will not only be unique, but it will be another chapter in a much larger story. Tradition doesn't have to be a trite, tired, exhausting thing. Mount Nittany is, literally, a living tradition right in our midst.

When we look at Mount Nittany, these different chapters in the same story are all visible at once. Jay Paterno sees Mount Nittany as a "symbol of eternity," and I think that's a really beautiful way to see it. When he looks upon it, he looks upon the same Mountain his father knew. When we look upon it, we see the same Mountain where Evan Pugh took the first students camping, and where so many generations over time have spent time.

We have a chance to feel each distinct story as a living and lively part of our common story.

TAS: We're nearing the end of our conversations on Mount Nittany and its story. As you state so well, conservation is a continuing effort—it's something that has to be carried on with each generation, or it falls apart. What is your message to the 17-year-old Penn State freshmen who has just arrived on campus?

BN: The lesson of both Mount Nittany and the Mount Nittany Conservancy for students is: Follow your heart. Even when you have to go against everybody.

One of the things we wanted to achieve with the Mount Nittany Conservancy was the perpetuation of the idea of the sacredness of the Mountain. I hoped that in giving talks across Centre County that the spirit might be felt decades later. The everyday work most of us do in our careers, in general, won't be felt decades after we're gone. With Mount Nittany—no matter your major or where you end up in life—you can identify with something that will still be beautiful and meaningful when you are old, and indeed will still be there *centuries* after you have gone. For those who, like so many today, don't believe in Heaven or an afterlife any longer, becoming a part of the ongoing story of Mount Nittany is the one chance many will have to become part of something that lives on. It costs you nothing, and asks only your admiration and reverence.

What is my message to the students of the 21st century? Learn the history, honor Mount Nittany as a sacred place, and realize that the entire story is an example of following your heart.

What motivated Fred Lewis Pattee to defend the natural state of the Mountain? What led Lion's Paw alumni on faith alone to commit themselves to protecting those 525 acres? What feelings led people to support our efforts to buy Willy Kogelmann's acres, or the cabin before that? In following the "whisperings of the heart" and acting on faith and intuition we as a whole people have conserved Mount Nittany. Whether you believe in spirit and magic and romance and legends, believe in one another. Believe that Mount Nittany is the story of touching hearts.

It's certainly touched my heart. It's hard to really properly put into words, but when I go up to State College it means so much to me to see the Mountain from the different views—particularly driving from Bellefonte to State College, because I often drove that way. Seeing the Mountain means so much to me, like looking upon a magic thing right in the center of the place where I live, right in the center of my life.

It's not that there's anything in the Nittany Valley's water, like people will sometimes say, that makes our place so special— rather, I think there's something in the Mountain that's doing it, some spirit that's whispering to our hearts.

In old dragon stories it was common for the dragon to lurk in the mountains and hills, to make his home in a place where he could dominate the people and take their treasure and sap their spirit. He was a force to be reckoned with, and he breathed fire as a weapon. Well, we believe there is something in our Mountain, too—but it's not an evil dragon.

In Mount Nittany a fire burns of a different kind; not like the deadly fire of a dragon but like the life-giving fire of the cabin hearths that once ensured the lives of pioneer-settlers. It is like the central flame from which a thousand torches can be lit. The spirit-fire burning in the Mountain is the source of the love that is kindled in our hearts during our time in the Nittany Valley. It calls us to its warmth and energy. It makes us burn brighter.

We can be like pioneers, because we can choose to keep the fire burning in the Nittany Valley by being conservators in our own time, fanning the embers in each generation.

Mount Nittany is the source of all of this; the source of our strength and spirit, a nurturer of our feeling for beauty, and the warmer of our spirit of friendship with one another. There is a spirit dwelling in the Mountain that both precedes and outlasts us—a spirit that lingers in the heart of our valley and in the hearts of each person who learns of it.

TAS: Dr. Novak, thank you for sharing so much of your knowledge of the history of Mount Nittany, and for conveying your own spirit and affection for the Mountain. I hope these conversations can be useful for future generations to understand a bit about Mount Nittany as both a symbol and as part of the Nittany Valley's landscape. Any final thoughts?

BN: I hope I've been a nurturer of feelings. I didn't start the love of Mount Nittany—that was present before me. Almost all the old-time Penn Staters I knew had a special feeling for Mount Nittany, although Mike Lynch was the living exemplar of it during most of my life. All I did was learn from them and Mike to love the Mountain. I still love it. I love to look at it and to climb it. I love everything about it. I hope others come to love it, too.

As long as Mount Nittany is there, Penn State will be there. If Mount Nittany ever goes, so the legend warns, the Wicked Wind of the North comes down and blows it all away. May Mount Nittany ever stand in our midst as breaker and shield against the destructive power of the winds of fate.

IV.
The Story of Hort Woods

In the course of this book I have suggested two central things about Mount Nittany. First, that its survival is the result of a "dynamic environmentalism" of both the physical and cultural landscape. And second, that it has become a symbol for the people of the Nittany Valley, and as such a tradition whose longevity will be determined by the extent to which future students, professors, townspeople, and alumni choose to live in the spirit of the tradition of the Mountain.

All this begs the question: what are the consequences for a static or limp environmentalism? What happens when a people chooses to reject or merely neglect living in the spirit of one of the Nittany Valley's traditional symbols?

The story of Hort Woods answers these questions. It is not a love story like the story of Mount Nittany. Rather, it is a tragedy. As a prelude to the story of Hort Woods, a bit of history about our Pennsylvania patrimony, and another woods, is relevant.

Our Commonwealth has for centuries been a special place of forests and trees. As Pennsylvanians we are, in fact, heirs of our founder William Penn's *sylvania*, which translated from Latin literally means that we're inheritors of Penn's "forest land." As it turns out, far from the Nittany Valley in Philadelphia, the Cradle of Liberty, lies a great and historic forest land still being passed along in trust from generation to generation.

The famous Fairmount Park covers more than 4,180 acres and runs through the heart of Philadelphia—although it is perhaps more accurate to say that the city has been built up around and even within what we today call Fairmount Park.

As the first major city park in America, it dates to 1812. As Philadelphia's University City Historical Society notes, Fairmount Park was "a pioneer effort in the conservation and ecology movement." Owned by the City of Philadelphia, its earliest formal purpose was as a source of clean water for the people the city—though it didn't receive official designation and protection until late in the 19th century.

The Independence Hall Association conveys the expansive and enthralling nature of Fairmount Park well in its short ode to the ancient, yet evergreen, forest:

"Every city touts its own beauties, but few cities anywhere can lay claim to the sylvan beauty on the banks of the Schuylkill River that are known as Fairmount Park. The Park is the largest landscaped park in the United States. We can walk, bicycle, rollerblade, or drive along Kelly and West River Drives today and feel ourselves deep in the country. In the depths of the Wissahickon Ravine and at other points in the park, the city's tall buildings are not visible over the treetops, and if it were not for the hum of traffic on the Drives, we could be in the pastoral world that Thomas Eakins painted. It was Eakins who immortalized the scullers on the Schuylkill—some of these paintings such as 'The Biglen Brothers Practicing' are exhibited today at the Philadelphia Museum of Art. The 'Mount' for which the park was named is the rise on which the museum stands."

"One of the world's largest municipal parks, Fairmount contains several million trees; the oldest zoo in the United States, Boathouse Row; cherry blossoms to rival those along D.C.'s Potomac Basin; Robin Hood Dell, an outdoor venue for soul-filled summer singers; the Mann Music Center, the Philadelphia Orchestra's (and others') summer amphitheater; picnic areas; tennis courts; miles of bicycle paths; bridle paths; an azalea garden; hundreds of statues and monuments; and two dozen or so 18th- and 19th-century buildings, which comprise an unusual historical patrimony."

What if Penn State had such a forest, like Philadelphia's Fairmount Park, running right through the center of campus? A woodland space so natural and dense that to stand in its center would be to escape even the modest hum of traffic on local streets, or sight of a campus building?

Once there was such a natural space in the midst of our University Park. Once there was such a natural endowment of virgin forest that even Mount Nittany might have to vie for a student's devotion. Its name was Hort Woods, and its natural endowments across time, its beauteous capital, was spent even in the same generation that Russell Clark, Bill Ulerich, and Lion's Paw began the work of conserving the Mountain.

While Hort Woods was nothing quite as expansive as

Fairmount Park's vast acreage, it was nonetheless a vast woodland space—far denser and far more remarkable than the lingering shadow of a woods that remains and bears its historical name. The Hort Woods of today, according to Penn State, runs from the "Park Avenue area south of the Arts Buildings (Forum) between the Beam Business Administration Building and North Allen Street Arts parking lot." It is a patch of woodland most noticeable when driving along Park Avenue, or walking north on campus toward the Nittany Lion Inn.

Steve Williams, managing editor of Penn State's AgScience Magazine in the College of Agricultural Sciences, has written of Hort Woods that, "It's easy to miss. I know people who have been at Penn State for decades and don't know about Hort Woods."

Indeed, Hort Woods was once something much greater. The Penn State Office of Physical Plant describes the historic Hort Woods, and what became of it:

"Historically this wood lot covered a very large area from Pollock Road to across Park Avenue to the north. In fact some remnants of this wood lot can still be seen on the north side of the Schreyer House. Hort Woods wood lot pre-dates the University, and was only cleared for its construction. Therefore many of the trees either pre-date the start of the University or are direct descendants of those trees. Because of its size and uniqueness on campus, Hort Woods has also become a special space and landmark on the campus."

The story of Hort Woods is a tragic one because it's the story of a conservationist consciousness that was stirred a century too late. While Mount Nittany is the obvious, visible symbol of the Nittany Valley, Hort Woods was once an obvious symbol of the campus—but one that became a casualty of a progressive spirit of building out the physical campus.

Hort Woods was destroyed not by any single action, but over the course of decades of whittling down—of taking just a few acres more—until something of a community struggle began in the late 1940s to preserve the forest from efforts by Penn State administration to clear-cut its final remaining, largest swaths for construction of parking lots, dormitories, and new buildings. It was a struggle that lasted for a generation, being occasionally picked up by professors, alumni, residents—but a struggle ultimately culminating in defeat in the 1960s.

While we know today, perhaps only with the benefit of hindsight, that in the fertile Nittany Valley there has always been plenty of room for the campus to grow—whether as far out as Innovation Park or through smarter reconstruction in the center of campus—it didn't seem so at the time when Hort Woods was slated for clear-cutting by Penn State administration.

In what turned out to be one of the final pleas for Hort Woods before the construction of the Arts & Humanities building, David L. Cowell wrote the following in 1961 to the *Centre Daily Times*: "It is a part of Penn State, a little sylvan which distinguishes our campus from Penn's, Pitt's and Temple's asphalt canyons. The Arts and Humanities building will contain man's art and music, but Shostakovich and Hindemith can't begin to uplift a man's soul like the Wood Thrush. Is there an artist who can match the inspiration of the Hort Woods tapestry in October?"

As it would turn out, the pleas of the mid-20th century

would go unheeded by a leadership whose eyes and ears were inaccessible to the message of Hort Woods' natural worth.

Yet the conservationist spirit that has animated the work of generations to conserve Mount Nittany would eventually take hold in a formal way more than a half century after much of Hort Woods had been lost.

In 2001 the Penn State Board of Trustees approved the passage of the "Heritage Trees and Groves" policy, directing the Office of Physical Plant's Tree Commission to protect the campus's most exceptional natural symbols.

"The campus environment is one of the top reasons students come to Penn State," declares Penn State's Heritage Trees website. "Although trees are recognized as vital to our campus environment, there are some trees that are more exceptional than most." As a result of immediate nominations in 2002 by Ryan Greeley and Derek Kalp, two Penn State landscape architects, "Hort Woods" and the "Hort Woods Remnant" are now enshrined as two of the eight Heritage Groves on campus.

While much of Hort Woods has been lost to the building up of the physical campus, what remains in our era of a renewed conservationist consciousness seems to be thriving. Campus plaques now mark its fringes, and improved stewardship of its interior and trails make a visit during the growth and heat of summer Arts Fest *de rigueur*. It seems we are finally beginning to learn an affection for Hort Woods that honors its historic beauty. A lingering spirit seems to be taking hold on the campus.

A natural wilderness amidst man's "asphalt canyons" can save us and uplift us just as surely as the song of the Wood Thrust uplifted the soul of David L. Cowell and his contemporaries. We have many beauty spots on the Penn State campus today—many finely managed green spaces, and lawns peered over by glass-fronted structures. Yet we have uncomfortably few genuinely wild spaces of the sort that Mount Nittany remains.

Our desire to *manage* beautiful things, rather than simply let them be—to "perfect" a Hort Woods with pavement, lighting, and chain-rails rather than simply let alone "a woods as a woods," to paraphrase an old professor—makes leisure an unleisurely enterprise. It turns a timeless experience into an historically-specific, man-created experience. It turns a relaxing thing into a self-conscious thing. It is the difference between nodding off anonymously under the shade of an Old Willow tree or having to sunbathe on Holmes Field in front of the peering glass eyes of the HUB-Robeson Center, or play with abandon in front of the massive glass expanses of the Millennium Science Complex or Business Building. We require spaces for the unkempt and natural that once entirely characterized our campus, if only so that a few small places remain where no little interior voice finds itself whispering, "*Who's this latest voyeur watching?*"

Our founders had such places of reprieve on Mount Nittany, and in Hort Woods. Our students once had such places of escape.

We know Evan Pugh would hike and camp on Mount Nittany. It isn't difficult to see him in the mind's eye strolling through the Hort Woods of his day, maybe smiling hand-in-hand with Rebecca Valentine, his beloved and devoted wife.

The Hort Woods "Ghost Walk" was one of campus's distinctive early 20th century spaces. It can still be seen in photographs hanging at The Tavern in downtown State College. One such photo tells us about this Hort Woods treasure in its a caption: "The Ghost Walk, a sort of lover's lane, was planted in 1858 by Professor William G. Waring, grandfather of Fred Waring. It was located north of the Zoology Building and extended some 200 feet."

The ghost of Atherton, perhaps, still lingers in the lingering forest of today. For that matter, Princess Nit-A-Nee and Lion's Paw and the spirits of the American Indians likely remain about the campus in its quieter, forgotten places.

It's more difficult to escape the peering, busy world today, but conservators can set about making it easier.

The destruction of the historic Hort Woods was essentially a failure of creative vision for the campus. It's always easy work to take, and much harder to keep or give. The work of building up Penn State and the Nittany Valley requires a creative vision in each generation of students, and among leading professors, alumni, and townspeople. The loss of Hort Woods was achieved over time. The work of building up a fresh inheritance is achieved over time, too.

The community record that comprises this chapter serves two purposes. First, it is a reminder of the spirit and feeling for Hort Woods that was ignored and lost. It acts, secondly, as a record that can guide our renewed conservationist spirit in passing along what remains as a living treasury for the future.

"A civilization flourishes," an ancient Greek proverb tells us, "when people plant trees under which they will never sit."

Let ours be a season for planting.

In a letter in Tuesday's *Collegian* the Hort Woods bobbed up again—a letter from alumnus and faculty member Harold E. Dickson. He pleads for the preservation of that woodland tract on North Campus "as is." "It is the last remaining portion of this campus to retain the wilder tag of a Penn State which has vanished," he wrote.

We string along with Harold on his principal contention, even though, unlike him, we seldom walk through those woods to enjoy wild beauties and delights; but we are not as sure as he seems to be that the way to preserve that area against "despoliation" is to keep it "untouchable." In its present "untouched" condition it looks like a forgotten or neglected portion of the campus, an area just waiting to be utilized for building purposes when somebody gets around to it.

Perhaps if it were allowed to be judiciously touched up, it might be more untouchable, if Harold can follow that reasoning.

Harold said further, "Only in Hort Woods can the leaves now fall in autumn to lie throughout the winter." Falling leaves have long made a perplexing problem for man—probably ever since the leaves first began to fall in the Garden of Eden. For our money, it is with leaves as with snow. Newly fallen, both are pleasing to the eye and to the feet; but later when weathered, dirty and matted down, both are ugly.

Harold may be pleased to know that for many years some members of the College Board of Trustees have stubbornly shared his views about Hort Woods. Now visiting his folklorish son Sam is E.S. Bayard, a onetime longtime trustee of the

College. Alternately offering sage advice or relieving tensions with robust stories and cogent wisecracks, Ed Bayard has attended more Trustees' formal and informal sessions than anybody else within this column's reading radius. If he wants to say anything, either sagacious or facetious, about the Hort Woods controversy, there is space in this column for him to do so.

November 20, 1948, H.E. Dickson, *Centre Daily Times*

An open letter to the Alumni Council and to the All-College Cabinet:

Many Penn State people—students, alumni, faculty—would like to see the "Hort Woods" area of our Campus preserved in a natural state. While there has been no announced intention of placing buildings in it, disturbing rumors to that effect keep cropping up. Nobody has said that buildings will not go there. Even now the largest of the trees in it are being felled with ominous frequency. In its way the situation is not unlike the forgotten case of Mt. Nittany when a landmark was saved from despoliation in the nick of time.

In the fall of 1921 students enthusiastically proposed branding the flank of Mt. Nittany with a huge S, either of whitewashed stones, or, as later suggested, of planted evergreens. Money was collected and the project was on the point of being carried through. But Fred Lewis Pattee, beloved teacher and author of the verses of "Alma Mater," publicly protested making a billboard of this "most distinctive feature of our landscape." Opposition was aroused, and the move was stopped. Other funds were afterward used to better purpose when the unscarred Mt. Nittany was purchased by Lion's Paw for the College.

I think Dr. Pattee today would agree that the Hort Woods tract, too, is worth preserving. It is the last remaining portion of this Campus to retain the wilder tang of Penn State which has vanished, but which he would remember. All the rest has been transformed into a well tended and landscaped suburban lawn on large scale. Only in Hort Woods can the leaves now fall in autumn to lie throughout the winter, instead of being scooped up by gasoline powered leaf rakers.

Preservation of this spot can only be assured by making it officially untouchable. All Penn State graduates and under-graduates might in some manner bring pressure to have these woods set aside and dedicated as a memorial grove—perhaps as a living memorial to soldiers, but in any case as one to an older Penn State. No funds would be needed. Little should be done to the place other than to keep it intact as a natural retreat for plant and animal life. But surely steps ought to be taken to do this before other irrevocable decisions are made and we are left holding nothing but regrets.

November 26, 1948, Mrs. A.W. Cowell, *Centre Daily Times*

To the Editor: Most colleges endeavor to have preserved on their campuses sections of wild woods as laboratories for Nature Education, forestry and zoology students. The Hort woods should be so considered. It is the last place on the campus for the bird watcher and the growth of the town removes other such places to impossible distances for the daily student of birds.

Except for a few woodpeckers, starlings and sparrows there are no birds in the Inn woods because food and shelter have been removed. The large trees in the Inn woods are dying as forest trees always do when the natural mulch is removed. The same would happen in the Hort woods should they be cleaned up.

I thought at one time that the very attractive new plantings on the campus would draw an increasing number of birds on migration. Such is not the case. Finding large numbers of species grows increasingly difficult except in the Hort woods.

Let us help Mr. Dickson in his effort to save these woods before it is too late.

November 27, 1948, H.H. Arnold, *Centre Daily Times*

First of two articles by H.H. Arnold of State College.

The Hort Woods is sometimes spoken of in a sentimental tone as a kind of antique, while at the same time it is regretfully designated a neglected woodlot or an unimproved part of the College campus. Much is being said these days about the conservation of natural resources. Is there anything in the woods worth preserving? What follows aims to be an inventory of the contents of this strip of woodland from the point of view of a nature lover.

Although Hort Woods cannot be called a fragment of "virgin forest", since it was completely cut over in the early history of the College and is consequently a second growth, still it must represent pretty nearly the native forest of this region, and the soil can hardly have been disturbed after the first cutting. The trees are now White Oaks and Scarlet Oaks in about equal proportions, with Black Oaks as a close third. Incidentally, one who has missed the coloring of the Scarlet Oaks along the drive and at the picnic ground this October has missed a real treat. Other trees are represented in the Woods in smaller numbers. There is quite a growth of young Locusts at the south corner, and in late May they are covered with fragrant blossoms. It may not be commonly known that in hot August afternoons the leaves also have a similar fragrance, as I have noticed many times in passing. The undergrowth in the Woods contains a great many seedling Wild Cherries, a few feet tall and in early spring these put out their delicate green while the branches above still seem dry and dead. The earliest green, however is that of the Ash-leaved Maples, of which there are several in the center of the Woods. The Wild Cherry, as well as the Sweet Cherry, are no doubt so well represented because of seeds dropped by the large flocks of blackbirds that come in the fall.

It is to be supposed that the Pines were better represented in the original forest, but there are now only a few left, an occasional Pitch Pine, a White Pine by the east walk, and another in the center. This tree provides a carpet of fallen needles and overshades a log for a resting place, that is usually adorned in fine weather with a couple of lovers.

Besides Red Maples (a fine one by the drive), and Mockernut Hickories, a number of species are represented by small trees or mere saplings: Flowering Dogwood, Alternate-leaved Dogwood, Walnut, Sassafras, Quaking Aspen, Bigtooth Poplar, Linden, and Tulip Tree.

Of the smaller trees, and the larger ones as well, the last to retain its green leaves in the fall is the Buckthorn. There are several of these, and it is also a common small tree in the woods north of State College, and in the uncultivated islands of the College farms. It seems likely that all these were planted by birds from berries gathered originally from a College nursery that is said to have occupied a section east of the present College mall. There is a venerable specimen of this tree at the end of the walk from Old Main toward the Home Economics building.

The Burnthorn is, then, most likely one of a group of trees that have escaped into the Hort Woods. Among other escapes, the most numerous seems to be the Norway Maple, then the Ash-leaved Maple, mentioned above, the Ailanthus (of A Tree Grows In Brooklyn fame), White Mulberry, Horse Chestnut, Catalpa, Kentucky Coffee Tree, and Alder Buckthorn (Rhamnus frangula), all coming quite clearly from parents of the Campus, and all coming from the dumping of raked leaves, twigs, and fruit. They are for the most part small, and badly overshaded by the native trees. In this group belongs a sapling of about twenty feet in height and two inches thick of an exotic tree called Zelkova (species serrata). We have seven of these trees on the campus, all large and flourishing, the largest just north of Main Engineering. It measures 10 feet, 11 inches, in girth and was photographed this summer by a tree enthusiast from Danill, a Dr. Baldwin. But that is another story. A few other saplings of the same species in the Hort Woods lead me to think the tree has escaped there and I begin to wonder if this East Asian tree has anywhere else taken to the wilds in our country.

In addition to the trees that have escaped into the Woods a number have been added by planting. Small Red Pines are scattered here and there and have grown very slowly, while the solid planting of this tree at the north center has thriven splendidly. They are now about thirty years old as can be determined by the successive whorls of branches. Near this same corner is a small planting of Pine Oaks. Along the edge of the Woods, Sugar Maples, White Birch and Red Bud have been set out in recent times.

The shrubs and vines of the Hort Woods may to some give it an unsightly appearance, but we should not forget that they serve as cover for the birds and chipmunks and also keep the fallen leaves in place as protection for the wild flowers. There are the usual and often annoying Blackberries, and also Raspberries, Elderberries, and even Wineberries and Wild Black Currants. The west side has an abundance of Sumac. Panicled Dogwood and Prairie Willow are found, and the Low Pale Blueberry, that we would expect to find no nearer than the Barrens of the mountains.

As you descend the path toward the Library, there are on the left several large bushes of Squaw Huckleberries. The berries are large and remain green, seeming never to ripen. But in September when they begin to fall from the plant they have a delicious flavor, not unlike gooseberries. For years the writer has had them all to himself.

By the end of June a low shrub called New Jersey Tea is found abundantly in bloom in the north part of the Woods. It is a feathery cluster of creamy white flowers. If the seed pods are gathered later for a winter bouquet, after a few days in the warmth of a room they contract and snap the seeds to a considerable distance.

November 29, 1948, H.H. Arnold, *Centre Daily Times*

Second of two articles by H.H. Arnold of State College.

Walkers on the north-south path will find the center of the Woods, near the White Pine, a large colony of the Japanese Knotweed. It is not properly a shrub, and dies down to the ground in winter leaving a multitude of hollow canes. Then it shoots up in the spring with remarkable vigor and speed reaching the height of about five feet.

As in the case of trees, a few shrubs seem to have escaped from the campus: Jet Bead, Bush Cranberry, and I have even found the common Garden Current, The Yews and Rhododendrons on the lower side must have been planted there, but Forsythia and Mock Orange farther back could have come from the dumping of refuse plants.

The vines of the Woods are the Riverbank Grape and the Virginia Creeper. The latter is especially abundant in the section neighboring the greenhouse. It offers the first red coloring in our autumn foliage.

If in the late autumn or earliest spring when the ground is free from snow, you should venture from the beaten path among the brambles, you would find several evergreen plants nestled among the leaves and moss. They are Wintergreen and Partridge Vine, each with their bright red berries. You will find too, Shinleaf and two species of Pipsissewa with their glossy leathery leaves. In June, these last have a pretty fragrant blossom about the size of a dime and shaped like a crown.

The early spring flowers, the ones that come while the trees are still bare, seem to prefer the sunny south-west side of the

Woods. Here you will find the Wind Flower or Rue Anemone, the Early Everlasting (that the children call Pussy Toes), the Early or Hispid Buttercup, Common Cinquefoil, and Blue-eyed Grass, that looks like a tiny iris on a spear of grass. On this side, too, there is an abundance of a plant called Heart Shaped Alexanders, a plant of the parsley family with very pretty thick leathery root leaves. Another plant of this family found in the same general section, but blooming much later, is the White Flowered Angelica.

As the leaves start out on the trees the spring flowers come on in quick succession. Bellwort and Smooth Solomon's Seal are common in the north-west section in the places where they have not been covered by a recent dumping of clay soil. There are a couple of colonies of the Wild Lily-of-the-Valley on the side toward the students' gardens. At about commencement time there is plenty of the Wild Geranium, the flower that blooms when the Wood Thrush sings. And an occasional specimen of the Four-leaved Milkweed may be found. This delicate flower, the earliest to bloom of the milkweeds, has a fragrance and a mysterious appeal that is hard to account for. Indeed, the charm of wild flowers in general seems to come from their clear cut individuality. They have style.

May I merely mention a few names. Readers will recognize old friends, and some may care to look them up in books. By mid-summer you may look for Saint John's Wort, Wild Onion, Goose Grass, Bush Honeysuckle, Carson Flower, etc. Bunch Flower is usually a cluster of lily like leaves that rarely puts up a flower stalk. Add Cow Wheat and two species of White Lettuce (Prenanthes).

By early July the Tick Trefoils begin to bloom. There are several species, the one called grandiflorum being our earliest. A little later you may find the small triangular pods sticking to your clothing. The species commonest in the Hort Woods is the one with the leaves on one stem and the flowers, and consequently the pods, on another entirely different leafless one, perhaps the better to deceive the unwary traveller.

August rains bring up the Indian Pipe or Ghost Flower. This small plant is entirely devoid of green and seems to be made all of wax. It impresses one as a rarity, and we are surprised to find that it is found over nearly all of North America as well as Japan and the Himalayas. And speaking of rarities, we have in the Hort Woods an orchid; Coral Root, a small inconspicuous thing, but an orchid none the less.

Our woods in late summer are likely to gleam with an abundance of the White Snake root, a shade-loving relative of the distasteful Boneset. With us it competes for space with the White Wood Aster, that is not very attractive individually, but effective in mass. There are also wide colonies of the root leaves of the Large Leaved Aster. These curious leaves sometime prove to be puzzling, for where the shade is dense they do not send up a flowering stem. It is possible that we should especially prize our colony of the Whorled or Mountain Aster. It is located where the paths cross at about the center of the Woods. I have seen this striking plant nowhere else near State College.

Of the Goldenrods we need only mention the one that is called Silver-Rod, and then the Wreath or Blue-stemmed Golden-rod. This one has none of the coarse structure usually associated with the type. As the name indicates the flowers are scattered in small clusters along a smooth blue stem. The Stout Ragged Goldenrod is a true giant. Gray lists it as "rather rare", but there are at least a dozen specimens on the slopes of the Woods facing the campus.

As in the case of the trees and shrubs some cultivated flowers have escaped into the Woods. I have found Lemon Lilies and Lilies of the Valley. On the left side of the path entering from the greenhouse road is a large area covered with a plant of the parsley family, Gout Weed or Garden Pest. It is quite attractive with its solid mass of green held late in the fall, but it may become a true pest in rock gardens.

A legitimate improvement of the Hort Woods might be the addition of a few missing species of our common wild flowers such as Blood Root, Wild Ginger, Columbine, Jack-in-the-Pulpit, etc., with a few of our common wood ferns: Polypody, Christmas fern, etc.

The writer is naturally alarmed at any talk of "improvements" for the Woods. There are always those who wish to convert it into a park. Evidently much more would be lost than gained. If we throw away our heritage the coming generations will arise and not call us blessed.

November 29, 1948, Editorial, *Centre Daily Times*

Spare That Oak

A lot of lively comment has been stirred up concerning the removal of trees on the College campus.

It all started with an editorial in the *Times*, bemoaning the fact that the campus was beginning to look like a city what with the new construction being jammed close to older buildings.

First came a semi-official protest from College authorities who pointed out that landscape experts approved their every move, that the College campus was considered among the most beautiful in the nation, and that the layman couldn't possibly know what he was talking about when it came to laying out an area from a tree and shrub standpoint.

Then came a very funny comment from the *Times'* town Bookworm, who announced the operation of a society called "Stoos," or "Spare That Old Oak." It's aim, Bookworm declared, was "to stop all building construction where any tree now stands."

Along about the same time, State College residents began writing letters. These appealed for the preservation of Hort Woods as one of the historic monuments on campus, a haven for nature lovers and a beauty not to be destroyed by progress.

It's all most interesting.

Although the original *Times* editorial asserted that the destroying of the trees to make way for new construction was a shame, it was not the major point of the article.

It simply pointed out that the College campus retain a rural touch, keeping in line with State College and Centre County, as opposed to the jam-packed skyscraper effect of a New York, Philadelphia or Pittsburgh institution of learning.

It appealed for a retention of the campus as it looks today—or looked a few years back—by spreading out rather than confining new construction to the boundaries of the campus as they are generally accepted.

That's strictly a personal observation from a layman—but one shared even by landscape architects, foresters and perhaps others who may know something about rural beauty.

Progress, of course, is considered essential for any community or organization or institution.

But if the College must continue its expansion—and the *Times* certainly is in favor of a bigger and better Penn State—let it be outward toward the mountains instead of inward toward Old Main.

December 22, 1948, C.A.H., *Centre Daily Times*

To the Editor: In the *Collegian* of Feb. 24, 1922, when Dr. Fred Lewis Pattee and others were making an effort to prevent students from marring the beauty of Mount Nittany, Arthur W. Cowell, then Professor of Landscape Architecture at the College, quoted the following poem:

Insult not Nature with absurd expense,
Nor spoil her simple charms by vain pretense;
Weigh well the subject, be with caution bold,
Profuse of genius, not profuse of gold.

The quotation is pertinent today in Harold Dickson's effort to save Hort Woods. Mr. Cowell is now chairman of the Planning Commission of the Borough of State College.

January 11, 1949, H.E. Dickson, *Centre Daily Times*

To the Editor: The damage that has been done to Hort Woods, as a natural site is already serious and irreparable, considering that 24 inch trees do not grow overnight. Walking the length of the plot you can count upwards of 50 stumps, and the number is increasing.

The woodchoppers are pretty busy in there nowadays, stacking up fuel for fireside sessions and laying out big freshly cut logs as seats for an unused and unneeded "outdoor chapel." I am told by authorities who have no axe to grind that most of this cutting is not really necessary, unless—and this is the disturbing possibility—unless the ultimate intention it to trim out all Hort Woods like a picnic grounds, or like the genteel grove of shade trees behind the Nittany Lion.

If and when that happens, the game will be over. Hort Woods can then go to blazes, as too much of it already has.

Sentimental considerations aside, this place in its present state fulfills a need. Professor Arnold's remarkable inventory has shown its botanical riches, and the area might well be stocked with additional specimens. Bird watchers know it as their only nearby hunting grounds. The College could enlist warmest support and approval for an announced decision to retain this last wild spot on the Campus as a convenient and useful nature laboratory. There are so many who wish that this decision might be forthcoming, and who most fervently wish that unemployed lumbermen might hereafter be exercised harmlessly on apparatus in Rec Hall.

December 13, 1949, H.E. Dickson, *Centre Daily Times*

To the Editor: Poor Hort Woods. The ax men are in there again, tidying up the place. Last year they lopped off lower branches to make a stand of pines at the northern corner look like a bed of telephone poles each with a Christmas tree on top.

Lately they've taken to cutting the saplings from wide swaths along the paths. Two whacks of an ax toppled a sassafras whose leaves have provided the first vivid spot of autumn color; a few more accounted for some locusts that used to perfume the air in blooming season.

I suppose underbrush is poisonous to landscapists with neatness fixations, but it belongs in the woods.

Suggestion: if those fellows must chop, turn them loose on the dummy wooden columns that clutter up the entrance lobby of the College Library. Good firewood there, boys.

December 15, 1949, T.H.C., *Centre Daily Times*

The ax men are at it again, and Harold Dickson is at it again. In Tuesday's paper he had a letter protesting acts of the ax men who are "tidying up" Hort Woods. Harold would leave that wooded tract as is, with underbrush, locusts and sassafras shrubs and everything. Every leaf, green or sere, every twig, every bush and every tree in those woods are dear to Harold's heart, pleasing to his eye, perfuming to his nose, easy on his feet, and altogether satisfying to his feeling for the artistic *au natural*—and we don't blame him a bit!

And we hope no prankster sends Harold a toy red ax for Christmas.

September 19, 1950, H.E. Dickson, *Centre Daily Times*

To the Editor: The College is still engaged in heavy lumbering operations, and I suppose nothing can stop it. But plenty of people don't like it.

Trees were chopped for a congestion of men's dormitories which some are saying ought to have been put in the open spaces of the outer Campus. Impending new buildings will cost more trees. A fine grove has been slaughtered for parking grounds behind the Nittany Lion Inn. Now the southern corner of Hort Woods has been earmarked—already staked out—for the same fate and purpose.

It was, after all, a pretty little stretch of road, that curve through the woods, even with parking space bitten off one side of it. And Hort Woods is a precious Penn State heritage, the last of its kind, worth preserving intact.

But somehow the bookkeepers don't seem to mind squandering that kind of capital.

March 26, 1952, Harold E. Dickson, Lament Over a Proposal to Pave a Parking Strip on the Southwest Side of Hort Woods

Submitted to the Centre County Penn State Alumni Club:

O why do they have to park in Hort Woods
Instead of in some other handy neighborhoods?
When a student wants to store his automobile for free
They say Mr. Trainer go fell a tree—or two or three.
Or when some car-riding prof has ceased to be limber
They say O let him park where there used to be timber

Where as a sylvan retreat for shy birdies the place isn't
    anymore the same
And there's need of traffic signals to protect small game.

Now trustee 'Casey' Jones, no other,
Announced there'll always be a Hort Woods, Brother.
And Ike's brother Milton said in a letter
We'll keep the woods, though it's all right to cut down
    sick trees to make them get better.
With choice botanical stuffs the grove will be stocked
And maybe here and there a rock garden will be rocked.
Which is OK so long as they don't plant pansy beds
Or get some other silly notions into their heads.
A woods is a woods is a woods,
Said G. Stein, and she had the goods.

This means that a woods is not a damned parking lot.
Or to put it another way, when covered with blacktop
    a forest it is not.
Gone isn't going; gone is GONE.
And if a strip northeast of Beaver Field is paved for parking
    it won't get to be Hort Woods again later on.
Suppose many a fellow who has got into a rut there does
    think he has rights of a squatter—
I say he's only doing that which he hadn't oughtter.
The encroaching plague of gas buggies is a leetle
Like the pestiferous Japanese beetle,
And I say to those who wish Hort Woods to come to no harm
Now is the time for all good men again to view with alarm.

June 17, 1961, David L. Cowell, *Centre Daily Times*

Save Hort Woods!

To the Editor: On Sunday the song of the Wood Thrush joyously filled Hort Woods for the first time this year. It was appropriate that one of nature's most accomplished musicians chose this day on which to begin his summer serenade.

In speaking about the thrush, Thoreau said, "The Thrush alone declares the immortal wealth and vigor that is in the forest. Here is a bird in whose strain the story is told ... Whenever a man hears it he is young and Nature is in her spring, wherever he hears it, it is a new world and a free country, and the gates of Heaven are not shut against him."

He was bravely singing again Monday, his flute-like tones almost drowned by the noise of the earth boring machines. The Humanities and the Arts are invading this small, wild place. Power saws and bulldozers will soon make short work of destroying the trees under which Atherton, Sparks, and the Penn State Yankee, among others, took their contemplative walks.

It seems a downright shame that Hort Woods has to go. It is a part of Penn State, a little sylvan which distinguishes our campus from Penn's, Pitt's and Temple's asphalt canyons. The Arts and Humanities building will contain man's art and music, but Shostakovich and Hindemith can't begin to uplift a man's soul like the Wood Thrush. Is there an artist who can match the inspiration of the Hort Woods tapestry in October?

There are plenty of other building sites. Penn State can have Arts, Humanities and Hort Woods. Sure, Hort Woods isn't much compared to Sequoia National Park. Neither is Central Park, but look what it does for New Yorkers!

When bulldozers bent on a misguided "improvement" attacked Thoreau's Walden Pond people and the Massachusetts courts came to the rescue. Will somebody save Hort Woods?

June 29, 1961, Julia Gregg Brill, *Centre Daily Times*

To the Editor: I was pleased to read in the June 17 issue of The *Times* David L. Cowell's plea that Hort Woods be saved as a distinctive feature of Penn State's campus and a haven for such shy songsters as the wood thrush. It is the only such plea I have seen in print since announcement was made last December that the Arts and Humanities Building would occupy the entire southern half of the Woods.

A number of us protested directly to the Administration in December and were given a detailed explanation of why the architects had chosen that site, what other sites had been considered and why each was rejected, and, in general, a view of the long-range building program of the University. It did not ease our unhappiness at the invasion of Hort Woods, but it did convince us that protest was useless.

We learned, however, that the five acres immediately adjacent to Park Ave. are not involved in present planning. On the theory that half a Wood is better than none at all, I have been centering my attention upon saving those five acres as a memorial to the Founders, since it is the only spot on campus which is today much as it was in 1855.

I have reason to believe that members of the School of Forestry would gladly undertake the rehabilitation of the wood-lot by planting young trees to replace the older ones when they die and must be removed and would maintain the plot as a small nature preserve.

Since some expense would be involved in maintaining the Wood, I and some of my friends have earmarked our contributions to the 1961 Alumni Fund "for the maintenance of Hort Woods as a Founders Memorial." (Memorials are more likely to survive than even irreplaceable works of art.) Monies so earmarked cannot be used for any other purpose without the consent of the donor and so will be a constant reminder, even though our project is not immediately accepted, that Hort Woods has friends to the very end.

The Alumni Fund does not close its books until June 30 and will immediately open them for the 1962 Fund. It is not too late for interested persons to swell the tiny sum we have deposited.

January 11, 1963, Daniel R. Clemson, *Centre Daily Times*

Hort Woods Yielding to New Construction: Arts and Humanities Project Progresses Following Operation to Preserve Forest

The planned removal of a tree is invariably accompanied by objections of some nature lovers and those opposed to changing status quo.

When authorization was given for the construction of a three-unit Arts and Humanities Center in Hort Woods on the

University campus, numerous pleas were heard for the preservation of the wooded area.

The project required the removal of more than 100 trees of varied sizes. Some students and faculty members alike called for retention of the woods in their present state.

This, of course, isn't the first time a wooded section of the campus had to give way to the continued growth of the University's physical plant.

Walter W. Trainer, now retired, who served for many years as head of the division of landscape planning, made a study of the campus' landscape.

He reported that in 1855, when the University was chartered, the campus was practically bare with the exception of a group of trees in the area of the Home Economics Building and a second growth of Oak trees, 12 to 15 feet high, along the northern part of the campus.

Hort Woods, which probably derived its name from the horticulture building (Weaver Building) after it was built in 1915, was a part of this grove, which extended south to Burrowes Building. A similar grove was located in the vicinity of the Nittany Lion Inn.

Trees from these groves were removed for the building of the Nittany Lion Inn, Pattee Library, Burrowes Building, Pond Laboratory and Frear Laboratory. The Helen Eakin Eisenhower Chapel was added to Hort Woods in 1955.

The Hort Woods site was chosen for the new buildings because a central location was considered essential for a unit of this type which will serve students from many different curricula. It was also desirable to locate the buildings near Sparks Building, Pattee Library and the new Chambers Building.

In all cases, efforts were made by the architects and landscaping personnel to preserve all the trees that were in good condition as a part of the landscape design for the center.

Total cost of the General State Authority project is $3,305,000. Excavation for the central unit of the three buildings has been completed.

The buildings will be located directly north of the Eisenhower Chapel and, as in the case of the chapel, the wooded area is expected to enhance the new buildings.

Two of the three brick structures will have two floors and partial basement, while the third unit will have one floor and partial basement. The exteriors are designed to maintain relationship by location, scale and material with the existing chapel and the setting of trees.

The architect for the project is Eshbach, Pullinger, Stevens and Bruder of Philadelphia, while the general construction contract is held by Gamble and Gamble Construction Company of Bolivar.

The Concept of integrated utilization was applied in the clearance of the site. In a few words, this means the practice of good woods use was applied to preserve the beauty of the location.

The project afforded Penn State's school of forestry an unintended opportunity to witness wood utilization practices recommended for the logging industry.

Although the construction project covers eight or nine acres of the woods, only three had to be completely cleared for the new units. Care was taken to retain portions of the forest for artistic and landscaping reasons.

This was the challenge facing James Srock, sawmill operator from Ramey in Clearfield County, when he began the logging operation on campus this past Fall. He was sub-contracted by the general contractor.

The project has been watched with interest by two staff members from the school of forestry: Orval A. Schmidt of the department of wood utilization and Merwin W. Humphrey of the department of forest management. Both agree that Mr. Srock's work conforms to advisable practices for contractors who must meet the costs of cutting trees and preparing logs.

The wooded area is predominantly Red Oak. Most trees of commercial size had already passed their peak of growth. Their most rapid growth occurred about 100 years ago when the then Farmer's High School was established.

About 30 years ago, a decline in growth took place, as evidenced by the stumps, according to Mr. Humphrey and Mr. Schmidt.

Mr. Srock is no stranger to the campus. During World War II, he was associated with the Navy V-12 program. Later he spent a year studying animal husbandry with the College of Agriculture.

Full use of forest trees is the goal of profitable management. The logger must decide which logs or bolts will bring him the highest return per cubic foot for various uses.

Mr. Srock says he believes "in making a few additional cuts to do the job right." The value of the product may be improved by cutting sections with the highest grade from the tree and combining defective portions with logs of lower quality.

Great care also was taken in removing trees on the margins of the actual site of the future buildings. In some instances, a crane was used to prevent a tree being removed from tilting against those being retained as scenery.

Differences exist between the practices employed by Mr. Srock in preparing the building site and those used on managed forest lands such as State forests.

Low stumps are normally required in order to make the most use of a tree and to eliminate the stump as an obstacle to logging equipment. On the campus job, high stumps were left in order to make removal easier.

In contrast to the necessary removal of stumps and limbwood from the totally cleared area, forestry practices include the retention of protective materials from logging for a variety of needs.

These vary from retention of water to maintaining a balance of natural conditions for biological and physical values. In some instances, however, materials are cleared from the soil to prevent forest fires or to encourage regeneration of tree species.

A chipping machine was used on the Penn State job to dispose of the limbwood. These machines are used in timber that needs thinning, for utilizing fallen and diseased trees and in areas where full-scale operations are impractical.

Cutting also calls for care in keeping to a minimum damage to trees reserved for borders and in areas which will become space between buildings.

For example, caution was exercised in protecting wooded areas virtually untouched by the clearing operation in order to assure continued growth.

In most cases, users of the materials from Hort Woods' trees will not be aware of the source of their product. However many students in the art school have acquired specimens to be made into works of art.

Many of them will use some chemical, such as polyethylene glycol-1000, to insure some stabilization and reduction of shrinkage as the specimens dry out.

Fourteen of the best logs were saved for the veneer market. As a finished product, the Oak veneer will be applied to furniture.

The bolt wood was cut to specifications and shipped to the West Virginia Pulp and Paper Company plant at Tyrone. There it will be merged with less significant strains of pulpwood.

Some of the firewood was only moved a few feet to the fireplace in back of the Eisenhower Chapel. Other firewood went to homes in the area.

The chipped wood, some of which was delivered to the horticulture department of the College of Agriculture to be used as a soil amendment, was sold locally to dairy farms for bedding material.

Still remaining at Hort Woods are many tall Red Oak trees— and memories of an area that has gradually yielded to the neverending growth of the University campus.

V.

Who Owns Mount Nittany?

Terry Dunkle

The following originally appeared in the July/August 1976 issue of Town and Gown. *It is the story of the personalities responsible for Mount Nittany's earliest formal preservation.*

This is a tale of men with a faith strong enough to move mountains, only in this case they used it to make one stay put.

A cold fall morning in 1945: Bill Ulerich '31 is sitting at his desk scanning today's edition of the *Centre Daily Times*. His office smells of ink and hot type. He blue-pencils a few errors in a story about Harry Truman and atom bombs, then flips inside to have a look at the legal ads. Suddenly he grabs for the phone.

"Operator, get me State College four-five-seven-one."

The operator patches him into the office of Russell Clark '19, chief scribe and stamp-licker for the alumni of Lion's Paw, a secret Penn State honor society to which Bill belongs.

"Russ," says Bill, "something big's come up. How much money do we have in the treasury?"

"Couple of hundred; why?"

"I noticed an ad here offering to sell Mount Nittany."

"Mount Nittany?"

"Yes."

"My God! Where would we hold initiations?"

"It's worse than that, Russ. They're offering timber rights, too."

There was a moment of silence.

"How much?" Russ finally asked.

"They don't give a price. Maybe you should ring up Army Armstrong. Wasn't he one of the owners?"

"Yes. I'll check right away."

Next morning Elliott M. "Army" Armstrong of Penn State's industrial engineering department and his partners in the Nittany Outing Club, J. Stanley Cobb '43 and Earl Grove, told Russell it was a good thing he'd called as soon as he had; lumber crews from West Virginia Pulp and Paper were moving in tomorrow morning. Army didn't want to see "The Mountain" spoiled any more than Russell did, but let's face it, he said, the Nittany Outing Club couldn't live on sentiment. They figured Lion's Paw was a perfect buyer, and all they wanted for their 517 acres was $2,000—not a bad price for a piece of land twice the size of Penn State's main campus.

"We don't have that kind of money and you know it," Russell said.

"Well, then," said Army, "be sure to listen for the chain saws tomorrow morning."

There was silence for a moment. Finally, Russell said, "I guess you fellows have us cornered. Have you got a pen?"

Russell hastily drew up, in his own name, an option to buy the mountain, and drafted a Lion's Paw check for $300 to seal the bargain. It was some minutes later, in Bill Ulerich's office, that the full import of what he'd done came clear to him. He got Bill to agree that if they had any trouble selling the idea to Lion's Paw alumni, they would complete the purchase themselves.

Today Bill Ulerich, president of Penn State's Board of Trustees, owns several newspapers and radio stations, but in those days he was earning less than $100 a week at the CDT, and "two thousand seemed like a lot of money," as he recalls. Russell Clark was in no better straits. To those who didn't understand Mount Nittany's significance to this area, the two brothers of the Paw had gone out on a limb just to save a few scraggly trees.

Mount Nittany occupies the prow of an 80-mile ridge jutting into the Centre Region from the Susquehanna near Lewisburg. Nearly everyone affiliated with Penn State or State College lives and works in her shadow. Part of her charm is that wherever we travel in the region she shows us a different face.

"If you wanted to," a visitor once told Lion's Paw alumnus

Ross Lehman '42, "you couldn't have placed that mountain in a better spot. It's just like God put it there."

Among local folks, feelings about Mount Nittany run deep, but outsiders sometimes scoff. Years ago, a few smart alecks who'd been to the Rockies came here and dubbed our august hill "Not-any Mountain." It's true that Mount Nittany refuses to tower over us, although with a little work some of us have managed to make it loom. A billion years ago, when the Rockies were only a gleam in the Creator's eye, Mount Nittany quite possibly scraped higher clouds than McKinley or Everest do today, but water and ice have scoured it down to 2,077 feet above sea level, or only 1,050 feet above the valley floor.

We can at least brag about the variety of trees on our mountain, whose forests include maple, oak, chestnut, butternut, wild cherry, aspen, walnut, and black birch. The cherry alone might have been worth the $2,000 except that the mountain had been stripped of timber about forty years earlier, and most of the trees were still only of pole girth.

Here and there on the mountain the new owners found signs of ancient farms, most of them abandoned generations earlier. The mountain had passed through many hands during the 200 years since the first claims were filed with the commonwealth. Most of it was first deeded in 1794 to Ross Johnston, and by the era of the Great Depression, the mountain was acquired by Army Armstrong and the Nittany Outing Club.

Most of the owners found Mount Nittany too ornery to cultivate except as hunting land. The mineral rights still belong to the hundreds of heirs of Christian Dale, wherever they are, but the rights are of little value unless someone finds a wondrous new use for sandstone.

That's the geologist's point of view—informative, but hardly inspiring. To the Indians, and to the poets and myth-makers of early Penn State, Mount Nittany was born not of a seismic belch but of the love of an Indian princess and the miracles of a benevolent God. Here's how the 1916 *LaVie* recounts the story:

Down in the valley lived an old warrior and his squaw. ... Frequently it happened that just when the maize they had planted was ready to reap, the north wind came ... and wrested it from them, so that in the long winter there was little to eat. ...

An Indian maid came down from her hilltop in the night and built a shield for them against the north wind. The old people saw with wonder the thing that she had done, and called her Nittany, which means "wind-breaker."

Then a great sickness came upon her, and she died, and the old warrior and his squaw mourned her, and they built a mound over the place where she lay. ...

Then in the night came the Great Spirit with thunderings and lightnings; the earth shook, great trees came crashing down, and the people were sore afraid. ...

When the dawn came, the people came forth and marveled; for in the place where they had builded the mound now rose a great mountain. And they called it Nittany, in honor of her who was called pious and good.

Then the yearbook editors added a significant twist to the famous legend:

> In this valley there rose the Great Mother, not of men but of the minds of men. To her came the young men from many mies, and she taught them the wisdom of times past, taught them the use of tools, taught them the arts of working. ... And her sons went out into the world and worked with the arts she had taught them and brought back to her honor and glory.

Mount Nittany occupied a special, matronly place in the hearts of thousands of youths who left their families and came up here from Philadelphia, Pittsburgh, and other distant towns to learn farming. If the professors of the 1860s were hard taskmasters, the bosom of Nittany seemed all the softer. She was a wise and gentle instructor who understood that boys are not quite men and that work must be rewarded with play. She taught each student the unassailable truth that to climb a mountain he must walk uphill. Then, at the summit, she bid him lie down on the mossy earth and sleep.

Many an old grad, recalling the Sunday outings of his youth, will tell you the best part of a Penn State football game is looking out through the open end of Beaver Stadium (it was built that way on purpose) and watching Mount Nittany light up gold in the afternoon sun.

An exchange student from the University of Cologne was so

inspired that in 1965 he named his newborn daughter Bettina Frederike Nittany Nurnberg, and promised she would study at Penn State when she reached college age. And in 1954, during an abortive movement to change the name of State College, the Committee of Fifty selected "Mount Nittany" as the most fitting label for the town.

Time has wedded the Nittany name to all sorts of institutions expressing the local spirit. We have a Mount Nittany church, a Nittany Mountain Summer, a Mountain View Hospital, a Nittany Lion Inn and the Penn State Nittany Lions. Many local businesses have appropriated the name. On foggy mornings, when Nittany hides her face from passing motorists, the signs along the road keep echoing her name.

Lion's Paw began its intimate acquaintance with Mount Nittany long before its 1945 purchase. Members are loath to reveal their secrets, but sneaky outsiders claim that every spring since 1908, alumni have hiked up Nittany's steep side after dark, leading a troupe of blindfolded seniors to an open spot near the summit. There, after a few secret incantations, the students' eyes are opened upon a breathtaking view of the lights of the village and campus flashing beneath their feet like jewels on a rumpled army blanket. It is a sight not easy to forget.

Each year Lion's Paw initiates a dozen or so senior men—and lately, women—who have made their marks in student government, on the college newspaper, or through some other display of leadership. Not surprisingly, many have gone on to earn fame in the world at large, among them Bill Ulerich and three other current trustees; several former trustee presidents; Senator Richard Schweiker '50; former Harvard football coach Dick

Harlow '12; David Dodds Henry '26, president emeritus of the University of Illinois; Herbert Longenecker '33, president emeritus of Tulane University; Pittsburgh industrialist Robert Ostermayer Sr. '17; and Donald W. Davis '42, president of the giant Stanley Works tool company.

Others gain renown right here at the foot of the mountain: Bob Higgins '18, former Penn State All-American and football coach; Ross Lehman and the late Ridge Riley '32, executive directors of the Alumni Association; Dutch Herman '12, historian and first Penn State basketball coach; local attorney Wayland Dunaway '33; John Brutzman '35, former managing editor of the Centre Daily Times; Bill Engel '40, associate director of Penn State's Office of Gifts and Endowments; and local physician and one-time champion Lion wrestler Jack Light '36, to name just a few.

Lion's Paw—which was almost called the "Keystone Senior Society" until someone thought up a better name—was founded in 1908 by six students, John Barnes, Bud Furst, Jimmy Acheson, "Posty" Postlewaite, Frank Simon and Dick Pennock. Their original aim was to foster better behavior among students, especially during annual class customs.

In the early years of this century, student scraps were so loud and violent that townspeople began calling the period of customs "hell week." Upperclassmen hooted and hollered through the town each night, tearing up sidewalks and plastering shop windows with hazing posters, often to a rousing racket of gunfire.

By 1945, however, two world wars had sobered even the most fractious of youths, and Lion's Paw members were left with no specific mission beyond debating the issues of the day and entertaining one another. Their meetings were held in "the lair," a big room on the fourth floor of Old Main outfitted with two davenports, a chess table, bookcases, and two cuspidors. A typical agenda read: "Good fellowship; bull session; pretzels; fresh (?), sweet (?), snappy cider; plenty of smokes; and a general good time!"

After two decades of shooting the breeze, Lion's Paw was more than ripe for a cause. Ulerich and Clark needed no slick talk to persuade its directors to take the mountain off their hands. Ridge Riley, always the devil's advocate, apparently chided Bill and Russell for their rashness, but it was all in fun, and when Jim Coogan '30, Dutch Hermann and Lou Bell '29 heard the idea they offered nothing but praise.

The matter was put to a vote at the next annual meeting of alumni. According to Russell's minutes, after Hap Frank '24 moved to keep the property, "so many seconded the motion that it was impossible to record the original seconder—there was no discussion—Dutch put the question and there was a veritable roar of 'ayes.'"

And so, on the evening of November 13, 1945, news of the sale of Mount Nittany went out to the rest of the world. In New York, readers of the Daily News snapped open their papers to a short item reading like this:

State College, Pa. (UP) — Legendary Mount Nittany, one of the mountains that tower over the campus of Pennsylvania State College, was spared the woodsman's ax today, and just in the nick of time. A student alumni organization, Lion's Paw, bought the summit for $2,000 just as a pulpwood crew prepared to begin stripping operations.

Similar stories showed up in the Omaha World Herald, the Covington (Ky.) Post, the Birmingham (Ala.) News, the Worcester (Mass) Gazette, and in dozens of newspapers elsewhere.

A good many barrels of ink had been spilled over an event not quite so complete as the newspapers implied. For one thing, the mountain hadn't been bought by Lion's Paw alumni at all, but by their secretary, Russell Clark. So far, only $300 had changed hands, and no one could be certain the members would chip in the rest.

The newspapers purveyed yet another, even bigger error, which has been kept secret until now: The story about the woodcutters was a hoax dreamed up by members of the Nittany Outing Club to assure quick sale of their land.

"We thought it would help if we scared people up a bit," club member Earl Grove explained recently. Two other members, J. Stanley Cobb and G. Guy Miller, have confirmed the ruse; the fourth partner, Army Armstrong, died in 1953.

Recently we blabbed the news of the Nittany Outing Club's little white lie to B.M. "Dutch" Hermann, who was president of Lion's Paw alumni in 1945. For a moment he was speechless. After some thought, he allowed that "they could have sold the mountain just as quickly without using a trick like that. At that price anybody would have thought it a bargain."

Bargain or not, Dutch took no chances that fall when he presented his case in a newsletter to the membership. In fact, he used a bit of bluffery himself, the old "Don't-ask-'em—tell-'em!" ploy: "YOU are now PART OWNER of the most famous geographical landmark affiliated with Penn State," his letter announced. "... P.S. Your contributions will be deductible from your income tax."

There wasn't exactly an avalanche of money. Dutch's newsletter went out two weeks before Christmas, and it was Memorial Day before the fund finally reached its $2,000 goal. Some members grumbled that the college itself should have bought the mountain, while a few others simply pleaded poverty. Except for one $100 contribution and a couple of $50 checks, virtually everyone gave $20 or less.

Mount Nittany was bought right after World War II, when the nation threw itself feverishly into the making of buildings, machines, highways, and babies. The same spirit prevailed among Lion's Paw alumni. The first question that seized them was what to do with their mountain. "Put up observation decks!" someone suggested at their plenary session in 1946. "Widen the trails!" others said. Still others chimed in, "Build a lodge!", "Benches!", "Fireplaces!", "How about picnic tables?"

Many of these pipe dreams were soon made official goals, but today, thirty years later, almost none has been completed. Just surveying the land and searching the deed (the tract was assembled from 37 different plots) have cost the group nearly $1,000—more than the average balance in its treasury most years.

Short of money but rich in sentiment, the new owners decided to proclaim Mount Nittany "a living monument to the dead of all wars" and to erect, at a suitable spot in the woods, a small monument bearing those words. Eventually, the monument idea was scuttled along with the picnic tables and the lodge. Since then, most members bent on "improvements" have decided it is wiser just to leave Nature alone. A park, after all, is never so holy as a forest.

It may come as a shock to some readers that fifty years ago a group of Penn Staters wanted to emblazon the face of Nittany with a colossal S, of stone or concrete, so that all who passed by might marvel at the glory of Old State. The idea caught fire in the fall of 1921 and waxed hotter and hotter until mid-February when Fred Lewis Pattee, the school's most respected man of letters, wrote this letter to the Collegian:

> The mountain is the most distinctive single object in our landscape, a dignified and impressive mass against our Shingletown and beyond ... and it has a melodious name that more and more is becoming a unique Penn State possession. To make a huge letter on the front of it, like a hideous scar, is to turn it into a sensational object and take away much of its poetry. It becomes not the sentinel at the extreme flank of the range overlooking the magnificent valley, but is turned into a mere bill board.

Thoroughly debunked, the S-mongers decided their money might better be contributed to the building of a campus gymnasium—our present-day Rec Hall.

There are certain kinds of people who, when faced with something that "just sits there," cannot rest until they find a use for it. For them, it is easier to carve a Mount Rushmore than to let the bluffs crumble how they may, or to build a Perth Amboy, New Jersey, where mineral springs once flowed unattended except by God and gravity. No one has proposed building oil refineries on Mount Nittany, or carving busts of George Atherton and Evan Pugh thereon, but over the years Lion's Paw has had to stave off at least half a dozen other attacks from the dreadnought Progress. Some were official acts of government or business, others fly-by-night ventures, like the one recalled for us by Mike Lynch '45, now head of the group's mountain committee:

"One day in the summer of 1960," he said, showing us the mountain from his third-floor office window, "some of us got to looking over there and saw this tall, skinny thing sticking up. Bob Koser and I and Randall Mattern [a surveyor] hiked up there and discovered some fellow had put up an eighty-five-foot television tower and was running a cable-TV system for people in Lemont. You see the problem: if we forced him to take it down, his customers would just get mad at us. Fortunately, it turned out that this guy's equipment, impressive though it looked, was about to be outmoded. Some electronics people told us microwaves would be coming in and he wouldn't last long. So we just kept quiet about it. He later took it down himself."

The TV tower never did make the papers, though several prominent newspapermen were Lion's Paw alumni and must have known all about it. It's been Lion's Paw's habit to lie low in matters like these. Several years ago, they discovered that Rockview state prison authorities had unintentionally appropriated six acres of their land and put a fence around it. Rather than making a fuss, the brothers of the Paw simply deeded the land to Rockview. As Mike explained it, "it would've cost a lot to prove their survey wrong and ours right, and anyway we knew the property was in good hands."

Rash, willful damaging of Nittany's beauty is about the only thing that has prompted Lion's Paw to put up its dukes in earnest. Some years aback, they received a tip that motorcyclists were ripping open the hiking trails, leaving them vulnerable to water erosion. A few days later, Mike happened to be on the mountain taking photographs when he suddenly heard a racket of trail bikes roaring up through the woods. "I hid behind a tree, and when they came along there I jumped out and took a picture," he recalled. "There were six of them. They called me every kind of son-of-a-bitch and everything. I said, what did they think they were doing up here on our property, and they said, 'We have permission from the State College Lions Club.' 'Lions Club, hell!' I said. We scutched them out and posted the place off-limits to motor vehicles."

Although they were plenty angry, the members refused to prosecute the cyclists. Lion's Paw has never maintained regular patrols against trespassers, either, because they don't consider anyone a trespasser unless he works some kind of destruction on the place. Anyone is free to hike or camp on the mountain, they say, so long as he doesn't chop down trees, dump trash, roll boulders down the slopes, set fires, or build shanties—all of which have been done.

To prevent more serious encroachments, usually at the hands of business or government, Lion's Paw has sometimes relied on the influence of alumni. It's surprising how many industrial and governmental groups have Lion's Paw alumni sitting somewhere within reach of top management. For example: In 1959 Lion's Paw got wind of a plan to string a 122,000-volt electric line across the north face of Nittany, taking a hundred-foot-wide right-of-way by eminent domain. The first protest came from Mike Lynch. "If you try to move in there," he warned West Penn, "you're going to have the wrath of the town, the students, and everybody else come down on you." The power company refused to budge, even after alumni and conservationists made a big stink about it in the papers. Then, when nearly everyone had abandoned the fight, the electric line was mysteriously shifted farther down the slope so that it ran across private properties in Lemont. Why the sudden change of heart? "This never got out," said Mike, "but it was a couple of our alumni who hold pretty high positions at West Penn. They talked to the engineers."

Naturally, while most people in the Centre Region were pleased with the outcome, a few Lemont homeowners, forced to live under the power lines, were outraged. "Lion's Paw property is private, the same as ours," their argument went, "and nobody lives up there, anyway. Why pick on us?" Others, including many Lion's Paw alumni, argue that it was better to blight a few back yards than to scar a piece of everyone's landscape. Mount Nittany, they say, is not private property; it is public property privately owned."

Fights like that have encouraged greater solidarity among Lion's Paw alumni. Like forged iron, the more hammering they take, the stronger they become. Two years ago when their property taxes suddenly leaped from $146 a year to $543, the adversity "caused an instant doubling of contributions—we got a thousand dollars almost overnight." said John Black '62, now secretary to Lion's Paw alumni.

John said the tax problem has caused a few members to revive the long-standing argument that the mountain be deeded to the University, thereby making it tax-exempt, but most members won't hear of it. As the late W.G. "Bill" Edwards '14 of Penn State's forestry department put it thirty years ago:

> "Alumni ... above all others, cherish the traditions and customs which have developed through the years. They are vitally interested in keeping them alive and handing them down from year to year. The college administrative personnel usually is not composed of alumni ... Such a body could not possibly understand the motives which prompted Lion's Paw to purchase the tract."

John predicted that whatever happens in the future, Lion's Paw alumni "will do anything in their power to keep the mountain, even at the risk of bankruptcy."

Mount Nittany isn't much good for farming, as early settlers found out, nor are her upper reaches prized yet as home sites. Selective cutting of her trees isn't likely to make anyone rich, either. Our mountain bears no oil, hides no diamonds or gold. The prospect of buying her would give goose bumps to none but the most sentimental of real estate agents. Nittany's value is not to be measured in dollars, but in the dark whisperings of the heart. She is our Plymouth Rock, our Old Faithful, our Cathedral of Rheims, our Gibraltar. "The moment we see Mount Nittany," as one old grad has said, "we know we are home."

Terry Dunkle (The Pennsylvania State University, Class of 1974, English) is a native of Jersey Shore, Pa. Mr. Dunkle served as Editor of *Town & Gown* from 1977 to 1979 and taught writing at Penn State from 1979 to 1982. He is now a businessman (www.dietpower.com) and editorial consultant (www.terrydunkle.com) living in Danbury, Connecticut. His wife, Mary Dunkle, was assistant director of Public Relations for Penn State in the early 1980s. She is now Vice President, Communications for the National Organization for Rare Disorders (www.rarediseases.org).

VI.

The Mount Nittany Conservancy

Ben Bronstein and Vince Verbeke

The following originally appeared in 2008 as part of Lion's Paw's Centennial celebration. In brief, it is the story of the formation and continuing work of the Mount Nittany Conservancy.

The Mount Nittany Conservancy was established by the Lion's Paw Alumni Association Board of Directors in 1981 in order to expand its efforts to preserve Mount Nittany as a symbol for Penn State and as a historic, scenic, environmental and recreational resource for the public.

The movement to form the Conservancy was triggered in 1975 when the Association was hit with a five-fold property tax increase as the result of a township reassessment program. At the time, the LPAA Board knew that some owners of neighboring land or others who coveted it posed a new, perhaps even imminent threat of defacement from lumbering or residential development. In the years since 1945 when Lion's Paw first purchased 525 acres preserving the view from campus, the price had grown from about four dollars per acre to $1,000. The LPAA Board realized that the inherently small number of Lion's Paw alumni would not be able to raise enough money among themselves to continue buying land, pay increasing taxes, and carry out conservation activities.

State College attorney Wayland F. Dunaway, III LP '33, prepared a study that concluded that the Association should establish itself as a tax-exempt organization able to solicit funds from the public or set up a separate organization for that purpose. Thus, the seed was planted for the Mount Nittany Conservancy. Another State College attorney, Benjamin J. Novak LP '65, then LPAA president, and Dunaway, subsequently completed the legal work that led to incorporation of the Conservancy in January 1981 and to IRS non-profit status in March 1982.

The 1980s. In 1985 the Conservancy bought its first land by taking over a 32.78-acre plot on which Lion's Paw had purchased an option from the Boal-Lee estate in 1979 to prevent others from buying it. The Conservancy paid the $32,000 purchase price. That year Novak also learned that Wilhelm Kogelmann was going to clear a tract that he owned next to the Lion's Paw property. Novak entered into negotiations that resulted in Kogelmann's donating 93 acres and selling another 120 to the Conservancy in 1985. The Conservancy then faced its biggest challenge—raising $120,000 to pay for this acreage. As first president and volunteer executive director, Novak began a fund-raising campaign aimed at Lion's Paw members and the State College community.

Two community members of the Conservancy Board, Mimi Barash Coppersmith, former president of the Penn State Board of Trustees, and Robert K. Zimmerman, played key roles in the community-wide campaign by contributing their personal talents and corporate resources from their advertising agency and radio stations, respectively. Contributions included $40,000 from the Richard King Mellon Foundation; $30,000 from the community, alumni, and students, including $5,000 from the Phi Psi 500; and $38,000 from Lion's Paw alumni. The final $5,000 that put the campaign over the top was donated by Penn State Trustee President Emeritus William K. Ulerich, LP '31, one of the original saviors of the Mountain exactly 40 years earlier. Some 1,100 individuals and organizations contributed to the campaign, which had also been endorsed by the University's Board of Trustees.

As part of the fund-raising effort, Novak convinced College Township officials in 1985 to designate a 20 ft. x 20 ft. piece of Conservancy land as a legal subdivision of 57,600 one-square-inch plots to be sold in the form of "Life Estate Deeds" by the Conservancy as fund-raising souvenirs. Today more than 2,025 people "own a piece" of the Conservancy land.

Also in 1985 the Mount Nittany Philatelic Society issued a special "collector's envelope" in recognition of the Conservancy campaign, technically known as a "cover." The envelope featured a Society-commissioned sketch of the Mountain, called a "cachet" by collectors, designed by a Penn State student. A special pictorial cancellation mark was authorized by the U.S. Postal Service, "Mt Nittany—Legend and Legacy." This appeared only on collectors' envelopes mailed from the State College Philatelic Exhibition on April 27, 1985 to all donors to the Conservancy.

The 1990s. The fundamental goal of the Conservancy is to preserve all of Nittany Mountain from 1,300 feet above sea level.

The Conservancy's last land purchase was the 61-acre Jarnagan/Gilliland estate in 1989 for $1,000 per acre, thus completing ownership of all property on the Boalsburg side of the Mountain from 1,700 feet above sea level to the top, as seen from the Mount Nittany Expressway (Rt. 322 Bypass).

With this purchase, the Conservancy and Lion's Paw had secured the entire cap of Mount Nittany from the 1,400-foot mark, as viewed from the campus, to as far as the State-owned lands of Rockview Penitentiary on the way to Bellefonte.

The Conservancy had increased its total holdings to 330 acres at a total cost of $213,000.

During the '90s, the Conservancy Board enhanced the organization's structure and operation. Richard S. Pirrotta LP '87, and past LPAA presidents Kenneth W. Reeves LP '83, and William A. Jaffe LP '60 served as Conservancy presidents. Past LPAA president Benjamin A Bronstein '61 became Conservancy president in 1999. They developed an increasingly active board and more efficient operations; improved communications with Friends (donors) of the Conservancy, Deedholders, neighbors, and University and local government officials; and built a firm foundation and strategy for refining and implementing the mission, goals, and activities for the 21st century.

In 1995 the Conservancy noted the 50th anniversary of Lion's Paw's "mountain-saving" purchase by mounting a capital campaign in the community and among Lion's Paw alumni. The campaign raised over $75,000, which was first used to pay off the remaining $32,750 mortgage on the 1989 land purchase. The balance, along with the annual campaign to Deedholders and Friends of the Conservancy, produced reserves of almost $100,000 to obtain additional land and enhance forest restoration, trail building and maintenance, and other environmental and recreational activities.

The Conservancy Board of Directors, as amended in the Bylaws in 1998, is composed of 21 members elected from among Lion's Paw alumni and community residents. The president of the Lion's Paw Alumni Association, one student member of the Lion's Paw Senior Society, and one expert in forest management from the Penn State faculty are automatic members of the Board. Emeritus Board members may be elected after nine years of service. They currently are Benjamin A. Bronstein LP '61, Mimi Barash Coppersmith, William A. Jaffe LP '60, Christopher Lee, Benson M. Lichtig LP '73, Ralph Mumma, Benjamin J. Novak LP '65, Joseph V. Paterno, Rich Pirrotta LP '87, Kenneth W. Reeves LP '83, Anne Riley, John T. Ryan, Jr. LP '34, William K. Ulerich LP '31, William L. Welch Jr., and Robert K. Zimmerman.

The New Millennium. The Conservancy began preparing for the next decade by initiating a strategic planning process and implementing a publicity campaign noting the Conservancy's 20th anniversary with Ben Bronstein LP '61 as president.

A new map/informational brochure was published and distribution expanded through placement by Centre County Convention and Visitors Bureau and reproduction on the website, www.mtnittany.org. The *Penn Stater* alumni magazine published a cover story, and *Town & Gown* magazine republished a past article on the founding of the Conservancy, plus a sidebar updating its activities. The *Centre Daily Times* carried a news article and editorials. Public service announcements were broadcast before and after Penn State football games by WMAJ and two sister stations. An article appeared in a game-day program and free display ads in the Penn State's football and basketball "annuals." Continuous visibility was obtained with the Mount Nittany observation plaza built by Penn State's Department of Athletics at the Conservancy's behest.

The Conservancy's first phone service was installed at the office of Clearwater Conservancy. A revamped and expanded, interactive website was established. It enables the public to pose questions and make contributions and purchase the famous deed to one square inch of Conservancy land.

In 1999, the Board began preparing for its long-term financial requirements in the new millennium by establishing the Mount Nittany Conservancy Endowment Fund at the Centre County Community Foundation. Requiring a minimum of $25,000, it was made possible by several major gifts from members of the Board. These monies are helping the Board to focus on developing and implementing long range plans to advance the Mountain's preservation, accessibility, use, and educational opportunities.

In 2004, the Board worked with a Department of Landscape Architecture class in the College of Arts and Architecture where the students created a "Nittany Valley Studio" project which identified conditions and potentials for Conservancy, Lion's Paw, and adjacent properties on the Mountain and in the surrounding valley. This included defining the state of the forest, scenic values, access and trail alternatives, trail maintenance and signage needs, connections to adjacent and regional systems, educational opportunities, and visibility issues. From these efforts, the Board has created a standing Master Plan committee that focuses the Board on how best to serve Mount Nittany and all its stakeholders.

Also in 2004, the Board updated the goals of its vision statement into four categories: 1. Gather information to better understand the land and people using the land. 2. Define a healthy environment and how to maintain it. 3. Identify potential friends of the Mountain and ways to harness their energy to benefit Conservancy goals. 4. Improve and maintain relationships with neighbors and the larger community. The Board has reached out to more Penn State student organizations, and the Interfraternity Council, Blue & White Society, Service Learning Coordinators, and Circle K, to name just a few, providing work groups for trail building, maintenance, and clean-up projects.

In 2007, the Conservancy and the Lion's Paw Alumni Association boards signed a memorandum of understanding under which the Conservancy is responsible for management of both tracts of land on the Mountain. With recreation as the principal use of the Mountain, especially with large numbers of hikers daily, trail and boundary marker maintenance and safety concerns continue to be of primary importance.

Also in 2007, the Board implemented a number of important initiatives to conserve Mount Nittany as the dominant and popular icon of Happy Valley. Among them were updating the Commonwealth's required Forest Management Plan, establishing a part-time Volunteer Coordinator position, working to increase the visibility of efforts of the Conservancy, and adopting the "Leave No Trace" principles to be honored by Mountain visitors.

A major threat to the Mountain's forest health and beauty occurred during the dry spring of 2007 with the explosion of the gypsy moth population in Centre County. Over 3,500 gypsy moth egg masses per acre were found over much of the Mountain, and only 250-500 egg masses per acre provide enough larvae to cause at least moderate defoliation the following year. The Board was successful in having all the Lion's Paw and Conservancy lands included in the Commonwealth's forestry spraying program. College Township advanced the funds for spraying before the payment deadline of mid-December 2007. Through the efforts of a fundraising campaign called "Mount Nittany Needs Us," the Board marshaled the support of community and alumni. The cost for spraying was $13,005. A major source of funds came from a matching challenge grant offered by the Centre County Community Foundation if the Conservancy raised $5,000 during April and May 2008. The campaign raised $6,630. Additional monies raised before and after the months of April and May allowed the Board to meet its obligation to the Township.

Forecasts by experts indicate that heavy gypsy moth infestations will be a continuing problem for the foreseeable future and will continue to require additional special funding beyond the Conservancy's regular operating budget. Donations can continue to be made at the Mount Nittany Conservancy, P.O. Box 334, State College, PA, 16804.

To learn more about Conservancy history and current activities, get a map of the trails and directions to the trailhead, or purchase a Life Estate Deed to one square inch of Conservancy land, visit www.mtnittany.org. For specific questions, contact the Board at info@mtnittany.org, or by calling (814) 237-0400, or writing the postal address above.

Current LP voting members of the Board are Vice-President Robert L. Andronici '66, Robert L. Frick '79, Gary L. Gentzler '60, Don S. Kline '67, Erich G. May '94, and Vincent C. Verbeke '82. Active emeritus members are Bronstein, Jaffe, and Reeves.

Mount Nittany Observation Plaza & Lion's Paw Historical Marker

Mount Nittany can be seen closer than ever before to the Nittany Lion fields and courts of play at the Mount Nittany Observation Plaza near Gate B of the Bryce Jordan Center, directly across from the entrance to the All-Sports Museum at Beaver Stadium.

The plaza features two sets of binoculars that allows viewing the Mountain as closely as if it were right on campus. Two permanent display maps show the lands, major trails, and overlooks maintained for public enjoyment by the Conservancy and the Lion's Paw Alumni Association. The displays also provide a trail map locator and directions to the trailhead on Mount Nittany Road in Lemont.

One set of binoculars is wheelchair accessible as well as suitable for use by small children. Both can be turned 180 degrees, but moving them just 90 degrees to the left brings another spectacular sight up close; there the Nittany Lion weathervane atop the southeast corner of Beaver Stadium can be appreciated in all its huge splendor.

A special feature of the plaza is one of the popular Penn State Alumni Association historical markers. It offers a captioned-sized explanation of how the Lion's Paw Alumni Association saved 525 acres of the Mountain in 1945 and later formed the Mount Nittany Conservancy as a land trust to acquire additional land and maintain the trails and trees as a public resource. At least twice the size of most of these markers, it also contains an early 20th century view of the Mountain and rural environment that was then State College as they could be seen from the same location.

The historical marker and the plaza were initiated by requests from the Conservancy Board of Directors. Both the Penn State Alumni Association and the Department of Athletics embraced the respective ideas and assumed the costs. The Office of Physical Plant designed and built the plaza. The timing was just right, with the latest expansion of the stadium and beautification of the surrounding grounds under way. Now, in no small way, Mount Nittany is part of those campus grounds.

VII.

Inspiriting the Mountain

The Legend of Mount Nittany

The following story appears in "The Legends of the Nittany Valley" and tells of the legendary origins of Mount Nittany. Of unknown authorship and date, it is included here as an example of the sort of folklore that American conservationist Henry W. Shoemaker believed had the power to "inspirit the land" as a means to draw upon a culture's feelings for its environment.

The famed Nittany Lion still strides the ledges and vales of the legendary Mount Nittany. It is as though he embodied the restless spirit of the mysterious Indian Princess Nit-A-Nee who gave her name to the Mountain, the Valley, and the Lion.

According to legend an old Indian warrior and his squaw once lived in the broad valley between the Tussey and Bald Eagle

Mountains. Each year the crops they planted were wrested from their fields by a wicked North Wind in the autumn before the harvest. The valley was being deserted in the face of this Wind until a mysterious Indian maiden appeared who taught the tribe to build shields to hold against the wicked winds of the North.

The appreciative Indian tribe called the maiden Nit-A-Nee, which means "wind-breaker," and made her their Princess.

This Indian Princess fell in love with a handsome Indian brave of the tribe called Lion's Paw. This fearless Brave was killed in a fierce battle with the wicked wind from the North after his shield was stolen from him while he slept.

When she heard of Lion's Paw's death, Princess Nit-A-Nee searched every hill and dale of the land until she found the fearless Indian Brave's body, still standing even after he had died. She enfolded him in her arms and carried his still erect body back to a place in the center of the Valley where she laid the strong Brave in his grave and built a mound of honor over his strength.

On the last night of the full moon, after she had finally raised the last of the soil and stone over his high mound, a terrible storm came up unleashing itself with thunder and lightening and the wailing of a horrendous wind from the depths of the earth. Every Indian in the Valley shuddered and all eyes were directed to the Indian Brave's high mound upon which the beautiful maiden Princess Nit-A-Nee was mounted with arms outstretched to touch the sources of the lightning bolts in the sky.

Through the night they watched with awe as the Indian Brave's burial mound grew and rose into a Mountain penetrating the center of the big valley between the two legs of the Tussey and Bald Eagle ridges. When the dawn finally came a huge Mountain was found standing erect in the center of the Valley.

A legend had been born. The mound and the maiden had given place to a Mountain, and standing on its summit was a Lion surrounded by eleven orphaned male cubs, each of whom had the courage of the fearless Indian Brave and the heart of the mysterious Indian Princess.

From that day forward every place in the valley was safe, and the wind wrested nothing from the fields on which these Lions strode as fearless heroes from the Mountain. The people of the Valley from that date forward knew only happiness and bounteous plenty.

In the fullness of time men came from across the farthest seas to build a college at the foot of this Mountain. The strength and courage of the students of this college became known far and wide. In memory of the fearless Indian Brave and the mysterious Indian Princess, the students of the college erected posts on a field and fought their way across this field as the North Wind had once ravaged the fields of the ancient Indian warrior and his squaw.

As each student learned the destructive power of the North Wind across the fields, he also learned the strength of the Princess known as Wind Breaker, called in her language Nit-A-Nee, and the courage unto death of the Indian Brave called Lion's Paw. As long as this strength and courage is known in the Valley, Mount Nittany will stand as a breaker against the wicked Wind of the North.

It is passed on from generation to generation that, as long as the fields of the Valley resound each year to the reenactments of the battles between the wicked North Wind and the Indian Brave, the people who live in the valley will be happy and prosperous and safe.

But if the reenactments ever stop, Mount Nittany will lose its strength and disappear, and the wicked Wind of the North will stream down through the valley between the legs of the Tussey and Bald Eagle ridges, searing the land, wresting away all that has been planted and grown there, and scattering the tribes who live there. All the warriors and squaws of the place will then have to abandon the Valley and seek their homes in other places and climes, and learn the customs and ways of strangers.

This is the legend of Mount Nittany. May it stand forever high and strong in our midst, our breaker against the harsh winds of destiny and fate which sweep down from the North, the source of fearless courage and deathless love, both father and mother of the games by which we live.

May Mount Nittany ever rise above us as the Guardian before the gates of Old Penn State. May the mysterious Indian Princess ever stand in our midst as breaker and shield against the destructive power of the winds of fate. And may the Nittany Lion's cubs forever join in the games which are the guarantee of the life of the land we love.

About the Author

Thomas A. Shakely is a writer, traveler, and erstwhile journalist. He has written for *National Review Online*, *The Huffington Post*, *First Things*, *StateCollege.com*, and has contributed to the quarterly journal *Academic Questions,* published by the National Association of Scholars. As a blogger he has written more than 150,000 words on his personal site. As a traveler he has visited 48 states and eight countries (including Cuba), has spent 24 hours aboard the New York City subway, and traveled Amtrak coast-to-coast, twice. As a journalist he covered the 2010 Pennsylvania midterms, and previously served as an editor for a defunct 100,000-circulation daily newspaper.

A resident of Philadelphia, he returns frequently to the Nittany Valley. As a student, he served as President & General Manager of The LION 90.7fm (WKPS) and served in the First Assembly of the University Park Undergraduate Association. He presently serves on the Board of Directors of The Nittany Valley Society and the Penn State Media Association, where he founded the Robert K. Zimmerman Endowment for student broadcasting.

An eighth-generation Pennsylvanian, he is a direct descendant of a Revolutionary War militiaman.

About the Publisher

The Nittany Valley Society fosters a spirit of community across time for Penn Staters, Central Pennsylvanians, and friends through a knowledge of our past, an appreciation for our present, and an affection for our spirit as a living treasury for our future. This finds expression through virtue, vigor, and soulfulness apparent in acts of honor, the cultivation of customs, and the Old State Spirit.

The Nittany Valley Society is a non-profit 501(c)(3) corporation in State College, Pennsylvania that serves as a cultural conservancy for the Nittany Valley, helping people to discover its many treasures and better share the story of this special place. Visit www.nittanyvalley.org to learn more and discover our other books, including:

The Legends of the Nittany Valley by Henry W. Shoemaker

The Pennsylvania State College 1853-1932 by Erwin W. Runkle

The Birth of the Craft Brew Revolution by Ben Novak

Is Penn State a Real University? by Ben Novak

Reminiscences of Dr. F.J. Pond by Francis J. Pond

Praise

"Thomas A. Shakely's thoroughgoing story, nominally about a mountain familiar to all Penn Staters, is more about the intangible spirit that over the past 70 years has motivated a coterie of alumni—now in its third generation—to protect and conserve this symbol of the University for all time to come. Within Mr. Shakely's narrative—which adopts and adapts other narratives about Mount Nittany from years past—is the larger meta-story of pride, determination, and action born of love, coming obstacles, threats, and challenges, to preserve the largest natural physical symbol of our alma mater. In contradistinction to the successful preservation of Mount Nittany, Mr. Shakely analyzes the diminution of another natural resource and symbol —Hort Woods, today a mere shadow of its former self."

Roger L. Williams

Executive Director, Penn State Alumni Association
Author, "The Origins of Federal Support for Higher Education: George W. Atherton and the Land-Grant Movement"

"A wonderful compendium of interesting details, stimulating tidbits, and informative morsels about the iconic symbol of Penn Staters everywhere—Mount Nittany. The glorious and little-known beginnings of the Mount Nittany Conservancy as told by the man who started it. If the passion of Princess Nittany beats within you, this book will immerse you in the history of how it got there. An encompassing work from someone who clearly bleeds not only the blue and white of Penn State, but also the brown and green of a vibrant Mount Nittany."

John Hook

President, The Mount Nittany Conservancy

"Thomas A. Shakely has given to future generations a wonderful history of both how and why Mount Nittany—'an ordinary Pennsylvania mountain'—came to be conserved for generations to come, and why that conservation matters. Through interviews, histories, and moving prose, Mr. Shakely brings the past, present, and future of Nit-A-Nee's monumental symbol to vivid life. And even as he weaves the tale of challenge and triumph for those seeking to keep our Mountain in its natural state, Mr. Shakely also tells the much larger story of how 'dynamic environmentalism' allows us to 'infuse our physical landscapes with a cultural depth sufficient to ensure the survival of both.' Pick it up, pass it along, and savor this wonderful and lively book."

Scott Paterno

"I, too, have fond memories and stories to tell of the heartfelt times that shaped my life while attending Penn State and living in Happy Valley. Thomas A. Shakely has, without knowing it, expressed my sentiments and 'remembrances past' with the same feeling—and in great detail—in telling the story of Mount Nittany, which is our common symbol. I share his passion. It's why I chose to settle here, to retire and live in the Spirit of the Nittany Valley once more."

Ray Papale

Member, Board of Directors of Rotary Club of State College

Penn State Class of 1974

Made in the USA
San Bernardino, CA
28 November 2013